# THE ZEND-AVESTA

or Persian Holy Scriptures

# THE ZEND-AVESTA

## Or Persian Holy Scriptures

by

**Charles F. Horne**

**The Book Tree**
**San Diego, California**

Originally published
1917 as part of *Sacred Books
and Early Literature of the East,
Vol. 7: Ancient Persia* by
Parke, Austin & Lipscomb, Inc.,
New York, NY

ISBN 978-1-58509-418-9

Published by
**The Book Tree**
San Diego, CA
www.thebooktree.com

We provide fascinating and educational products to help awaken the public
to new ideas and information that would not be available otherwise.
Call 1 (800) 700-8733 for our FREE BOOK TREE CATALOG.

ZOROASTER
—MAGI—
1000 B.C.

Deep in conversation, an astronomer (Zoroaster) and geographer (Ptolemy) are standing in a group to which Raphael himself belongs. He is the young man looking directly at the observer.

# THE ANCIENT AVESTAN TONGUE
## (2000?–600 B. C.)

# THE ZEND-AVESTA

# THE GATHAS

"*Which of the two — that which the righteous or the wicked believes — which is the greater?*"

— GATHA AHUNAVAITI.

"*The mental heaven and hell with which we are now familiar as the only future states recognized by intelligent people, thoughts which, despite their familiarity, can never lose their importance, are not only used and expressed in the Gathas, but expressed there, so far as we are aware, for the first time.*"

— L. H. MILLS.

# THE GATHAS

THE word " Gatha " means " a song," and especially an historical song, preserving a tale of the past. We have already noted the great importance of the Gathas as being the only surviving literature of the earliest Persian language, the only remaining fragments of the actual teachings of the sage Zoroaster. In the present Avesta or Holy Scriptures as preserved for us by the Parsis, there are five of these Gathas included in a collection of other and much later Yasnas or hymns. Among these, the Gathas can easily be discriminated by their older language. The first and longest Gatha, as these songs now exist, contains seven Yasnas or hymns, the second and third Gathas each contain four, and the remaining Gathas only one apiece. As to the original form and order of these ancient hymns, we can only say quite positively that it differed from their present arrangement; because that has obviously been adapted to fit the ceremonies of the priests in which they are now employed. Scholars have attempted some rearrangement of the hymns. We can judge that what is now called the 29th Yasna may have been originally the first Gathic hymn. At least, it tells of the origin of Zoroaster's religion. Hence in our volume we place it first, to give the reader the opening view of this remarkable faith. The 31st Yasna, which is also an early one, is given next. Its translation has been specially prepared so as to retain something of the natural rhythm of the Gathas, and it will serve to show the reader what their chanted Parsi form resembles. The other Gathic hymns are then given in their present Avestan sequence.

The language of the Gathas is so crusted with age that even in translation their sense is not easily followed. The reader therefore may welcome a brief summary of what our scholars have deduced from them.   First as to Zoroaster himself, or Zarathushtra as the Avesta names him, the Gathas seem sometimes his own voice, sometimes the voices of his followers, but always they are very close to him in time and spirit.   They show us the man Zarathushtra as he lived, his hopes and fears, his wonderment as ideas came to him, his rage against his foes.   As to the date of the great teacher's life, the Gathas remain vague, and there has been much argument among our scholars, but no positive decision.   The chief American authority, Professor Jackson, inclines to the view that the sage taught about 600 B.C.   The date certainly can not be later, and some scholars would set it earlier by many centuries, perhaps even as early as 2000 B.C.

Zarathushtra was a member of the aristocracy of his community, in which an invading Aryan folk ruled over a peasantry of Asiatic, perhaps ancient Indian, stock.   In this already complex realm, Zarathushtra became the champion of peace as against war.   He urged his people to take up the toil of husbandry, the peaceful raising of cattle, instead of seeking the excitement of rapine, the plundering of the herds of others.   He taught the nobles that their God, the long-established Aryan god, Ahura Mazda, or the Lord Mazda, demanded of them that they should thus help and guide their subject-people, instead of destroying them.   Indeed, Zarathushtra looked far beyond that immediate item of dispute. He preached that all existence was a mighty struggle against the forces of evil, the enemies of Mazda, chief among whom was the Druj, which seems to mean the Lie, or falsity in general.   In this eternal battle of good and evil, all men took part whether they would or no.   Whoever was not openly fighting on the side of Mazda was thereby aiding the Druj.

Chiefly, though, the new teacher's religion centered about the cattle.   He spoke to herdsmen.   The Aryans must cease to be marauders; they must raise cattle instead of capturing them, protect them instead of destroying them.   He pictures earth itself under the figure of a cow giving bounteous supplies. The force which we call Nature, Zarathushtra names the " Ox-soul." Simple as his teaching is, it is amazingly modern in its clear concepts and high thought. The prophet sees but one god, though speaking often of what he calls the " Amshaspands," or attributes of Mazda. These are six: " Vohu Manah," Good Thought or Kindliness; " Asha," Right; " Spenta Armaiti," Piety or Harmony; " Haurvatat," Salvation; " Ameretat," Wisdom, or perhaps Immortality; and " Xsathra," Sovereignty. There is also a spirit or messenger angel, Sraosha or Obedience.

These spirits will be met with constantly in the Gathas; yet they are scarcely separate beings. The prophet sees them only as abstractions, voices of the Lord Mazda in one attitude or another. Indeed, even as late as the days of the Greeks, the historian Herodotus could still say of the Persians: " It is not customary among them to have idols made, temples built, and altars erected; they even upbraid with folly those who do so. I can account for that, only from their not believing that the gods are like men as the Hellenes do."

One can imagine that this straightforward teaching of kindliness combined with this abstruse and modern conception that even heaven and hell are only of the spirit, intellectual rather than material existences, found little favor among Zarathushtra's wild kinsfolk. They must, however, have felt deeply the appeal of his thrilling picture of existence as an eternal battle against evil; for it was this part of his religion which grew with later ages. The evil principle, the Lie, was given what it hardly receives in the Gathas, a name of its own. It became " Ahriman," or the enemy; and the later Zoroastrian books speak constantly of a dual creation, the war of Ahura Mazda (or Ormazd) against Ahriman.

At first Zarathushtra's teaching encountered serious opposition, but at length a mighty noble, Frashaoshtra, became his champion; and he wedded Frashaoshtra's daughter, Hvovi. Then their king, Vishtaspa, was converted; and we find the closing hymns of the Gathas depicting Zoroaster as in full power over the religion of his race.

# THE GATHAS

## I

## THE GATHA AHUNAVAITI [1]

YASNA XXIX [2]

1. Unto you [3] wailed the Ox-soul. [4] "For whom [5] did ye fashion me? Who created me? Violence [6] and rapine hath oppressed me, and outrage and might. I have no other herdsmen than you: prepare for me then the blessings of pasture."

2. Then the Ox-Creator [7] asked of the Right: [8] "Hast thou a judge for the Ox, that ye may be able to appoint him

---

[1] This Gatha is so called because its opening theme is like that of the chief Parsi prayer called the "Ahuna Vairya."

[2] Of the seven Yasnas or hymns in this Gatha, number XXIX is by the Parsis placed second, but it fits much more appropriately as the opening. (See introduction.) Its theme is the selection of Zarathushtra for his mission as prophet and teacher. The Ox-soul and the Pregnant Cow, or Nature and Earth, appeal to Mazda for protection against the destruction wrought by ravaging bands, who slay the cattle and (perhaps) destroy the crops. Mazda thereon assigns Zarathushtra to check this disorder. The ox and cow protest; he is too weak and unnoted a man; they want a king. But Zarathushtra at once accepts his mission with such energy that they are content. This Yasna is from the translation by L. H. Mills.

[3] Ahura with the Amshaspands around him. See introduction for these names.

[4] The Ox-soul is a being with much the same relation to cattle on earth that the Fravashis have to men. He complains in the heavenly council of violence done to those on earth whom he represents.

[5] "What" seems less likely. The masculine anticipates the answer that the hymn will supply.

[6] Aesmo, but it is not yet a proper name: it is on the same footing as the synonyms following.

[7] It is suggested that this genius replaces Mithra. He is not Ahura Mazda, for he addresses him in this hymn.

[8] The Right-Asha.

zealous tendance as well as fodder?  Whom do ye will to be
his lord, who may drive off violence together with the
followers of the Lie?"[9]

3. To him the Right replied:[10] "There is for the Ox no
helper that can keep harm away.  Those yonder[11] have no
knowledge how right-doers act toward the lowly."

(*The Ox-Creator*) "Strongest of beings is he to whose
help I come at call."

4. (*Asha*) "Mazda knoweth best the purposes that have
been wrought already by demons and by mortals, and that
shall be wrought hereafter.  He, Ahura, is the decider.  So
shall it be as he shall will."

5. (*The Ox-Creator*[12]) "To Ahura with outspread hands
we twain would pray, my soul and that of the pregnant Cow,
so that we twain urge Mazda with entreaties:  Destruction
is not for the right-living nor for the cattle-tender, at hands
of the Liars."

6. Then spake Ahura Mazda himself, who knows the laws,
with wisdom: "There is found no lord or judge[13] according
to the Right Order; for the Creator hath formed thee for the
cattle-tender and the farmer.[14]

7. This ordinance about the fat[15] hath Ahura Mazda, one
in will with the Right, created for the cattle, and the milk
for them that crave nourishment, by his command, the holy
one.

[9] *Dregvant*, "one who has the *Druj*," the standing antithesis to
*asavant*, "one who has Asha."

[10] Asha, as guardian of things as they should be.  But the passage is
significant in that even Asha is not high enough for the purpose pres-
ently disclosed.  Nothing less than Mazda's own commission will be
authority enough for Zarathushtra.

[11] *I.e.*, men below.

[12] But instead of him we seem to have the Ox-soul again, who speaks
for a primeval pair, ox and cow, or Nature and the Earth.

[13] *Ahu* and *ratu* are correlative terms, in the Gathas, denoting the
prince and the judge respectively, the former executing the judge's
decisions.  At the final judgment Mazda is *ahu* and Zarathushtra *ratu*.

[14] The cattle are chattels, and can only appear by their patron.

[15] Mazda declares that the cattle are divinely appointed to give flesh
and milk to men.  Cattle were the special province of Vohu Manah, but
the Gathas do not emphasize it.

(*The Ox and Cow*) " Whom hast thou, O Good Thought,[16] among men who may care for us twain ? "

8. (*Vohu Manah*) " He is known to me here who alone hath heard our commands, even Zarathushtra Spitama: he willeth to make known our thoughts, O Mazda, and those of the Right. So let us bestow on him charm of speech."

9. Then the Ox-Soul lamented: " That I must be content with the ineffectual word of an impotent man for my protector, when I wish for one that commands mightily! When ever shall there be one who shall give him (the Ox) effectual help ? "

10. (*Zarathushtra*) " Do ye, O Ahura, grant them strength, O Right, and that Dominion, O Good Thought, whereby he (the protector) can produce good dwellings and peace. I also have realized thee, Mazda, as first discoverer of this.

11. " Where are Right and Good Thought and Dominion ? So, ye men, acknowledge me, for instruction, Mazda, for the great society." [17]

(*The Ox and Cow*) " O Ahura, now is help ours: we will be ready to serve those that are of you." [18]

### YASNA XXXI [19]

#### 1.

Having in mind your doctrines (ye Gods),
we speak forth words heard not
by those who through the doctrines of the Druj (Satan or the
 Lie)

[16] Good Thought is but the translation of *Vohu Manah*. Good Thought is an attribute of Mazda.

[17] A rather problematic word, taken by Bartholomae as Zarathushtra's name for his community of followers.

[18] *Yusmavant*, literally, " like you," apparently means " you of the heavenly company," Mazda and the spirits with him.

[19] The revision of this noted Yasna has been made by Prof. A. V. W. Jackson specially for this series, to show what was probably the rhythmic spirit of the Gathas.

This Yasna might well be regarded as the first public speech of Zarathushtra. In it he announces his mission and asks Mazda for aid. In the ninth stanza he announces the choice made by the ox and cow in Yasna xxix and then questions what choice of life men should make.

destroy the beings of Asha (Righteousness),
but words which are most excellent for those
who devote their hearts unto Mazda.

### 2.

Since, owing to these things,
the better path for the soul is not in sight,
then I am come unto you all
a judge — as Ahura Mazda knows —
between the two parties, that we may live
according to Right.[20]

### 3.

What joy Thou wilt give through Thy Spirit and Thy Fire,
the united pair — and through Asha promisest —
as Thy decree for the wise in heart,
this speak Thou unto us, that we may know it,
with the word of Thy mouth, O Mazda,
in order that I may convert all men living.

### 4.

If Asha (Righteousness) be strong,
and the Ahura Mazdas too,
and also Ashi and Armaiti (Harmony and Piety),
then through the Best Mind I will implore
for myself the mighty Power
by whose force we may overcome the Druj.

### 5.

This do Thou tell me, that I may discern it,
know it through Thy Good Mind and lay it to heart,
what ye through Asha will give me as the better lot,
of which portion they envy me.
Aye those things, tell me, Ahura Mazda,
which shall not be or shall be.

---

[20] The word here translated "Right" is "Asha." The speaker seems
to pass indifferently between using this as a common and as a proper
noun. To him the doctrine of righteousness and the spirit Asha are one.
The two parties mentioned are of Right and Wrong.

### 6.

The Best (Heaven) shall be his
who, knowing it, can tell to me the very
word of Righteousness in reference to
the Eternal Welfare and Immortality.
Yea, the Kingdom of Mazda shall he his
which his Good Mind will increase for Him.

### 7.

Mazda who, in the beginning, conceived the thought —
" The Blessed Realms shall fill with light "—
He by His wisdom founder of Righteousness (the Law),
by which to keep up His Best Mind (in His people);
these Blessed Realms mayest Thou with Thy Spirit increase,
Thou, O Ahura Mazda, who art even until now and forever
       unchanging.

### 8.

Therefore in the beginning, O Mazda,
I conceived Thee in mind to be worthy of worship,
when I beheld Thee in mine eye,
as the Father of the Good Mind,
the very Founder of Asha, the Law of Righteousness,
the Lord amid the deeds of life.

### 9.

Thine was Armaiti (Harmony and Piety).
Thine, indeed, was the Wisdom of the Spirit Geushtashan
(Creator of the Cow), O Mazda Ahura,
when Thou for her (the Cow) laidst open the way
either to leave the husbandman
or him who is not a husbandman.

### 10.

Then of these two, she chose
for herself the thrifty husbandman,

as righteous lord, Ahura the Righteous,
the one that is promoter of the Good Mind.
The man who is not a husbandman, O Mazda,
shall enjoy, even though he strive for it,[21] no good report.

### 11.

When Thou, O Mazda, in the beginning
didst create our beings and our consciences,
and our intellects through Thine Own Mind —
when Thou madest life clothed with a body
when Thou madest deeds and teachings
whereby one freely may express his beliefs —

### 12.

So lifts up his voice alike
the false speaker and the true speaker,
the foolish and the wise,
according to his heart and mind;
but Armaiti (Piety), following ever after
with the Spirit, inquires wherever faltering may be.

### 13.

What open or secret things, O Mazda,
she judgingly inquires into in her search,
or when, on the other hand, for a slight sin
one demands the greatest penalty —
all these in Thine eye, O Glancing One,
Guardian with Righteousness Thou seest.

### 14.

Therefore I ask Thee, O Ahura,
that is coming and is to come —

[21] The Pahlavi tradition, perhaps rightly, sees in the Avestan word
*davans-cina*, here translated "even though he strive for it," rather a
proper name "Davans," or "Davanos," a king who did only one good
deed in life by kicking a bunch of hay before a hungry ox, and was therefore rewarded in Hell by having his right foot freed from the flame that
burned the rest of his body.

what claims in accordance with the records
are appointed for the righteous,
and what for the wicked;
And how these will be when in the balanced reckoning.


### 15.

I ask Thee about this, what wrath awaits
him who advances the power
for the wicked one of evil deeds, O Ahura,
who can not find his livelihood
without harm to the flocks and men
of the husbandman who does no harm.


### 16.

About this I ask Thee, how and when
and by what deeds, he who being wise
devotes himself to advancing
through righteousness the power
of the house, the district, and the land —
shall become even as Thou, O Ahura.


### 17.

Which of the two — that which the righteous
or the wicked believes — which is the greater?
Let the enlightened to the enlightened speak,
nor let the unenlightened deceive.
Be thou to us, O Ahura Mazda,
the revealer of Thy Good Mind.


### 18.

Let no one of you harken unto
the words and commandments of the wicked,
for he (the wicked) will bring house,
village, district, and land
into distress and death.
Therefore smite all such with the weapon!

### 19.

But give ear to him who has conceived
what is Right, an enlightened healer of the world, O Ahura,
who will have power at will over the words
of his tongue — so that they will be verified
through Thy red Fire, O Mazda, in Thy good kingdom,
at the Dispensation (Judgment) of the two parties (the
    righteous and the unrighteous).

### 20.

Whosoever comes over to the Righteous One,
for him hereafter will be remote
the long duration of misery, of darkness,
the evil food and woeful words —
Such is that life to which, O ye wicked,
your conscience through your own deeds will lead you.

### 21.

May Ahura Mazda, then,
out of His rich store grant
Unity with Weal and Immortality,
with His Righteousness and Power —
aye, the full enjoyment of the Good Mind,
to him who is faithful to Him in word and deed.

### 22.

Clear are these things to the wise
as to one who has conceived it in his mind;
it is he that in word and deed
promotes Righteousness with the Good Kingdom;
it is he, O Mazda, that will be
to Thee a most active servant.

#### YASNA XXVIII [22]

1. With outspread hands in petition for that help, O

[22] This Yasna, although placed by the Parsis first in the Gathas, is obviously of late date in the prophet's life. King Vishtaspa is his friend, and his power is high. This and the following Yasnas are from the translation of Prof. J. H. Moulton in his " Early Zoroastrianism."

Mazda, first of all things I will pray for the works of the holy spirit, O thou the Right, whereby I may please the will of Good Thought and the Ox-soul.[23]

2. I who would serve you, O Mazda Ahura and Good Thought — do ye give through the Right the blessings of both worlds, the bodily and that of Thought, which set the faithful in felicity.

3. I who would praise you, as never before, Right, and Good Thought, and Mazda Ahura, and those for whom Piety makes an imperishable Dominion grow: come ye to my help at my call.

4. I who have set my heart on watching over the soul,[24] in union with Good Thought, and as knowing the rewards of Mazda Ahura for our works, will, while I have power and strength, teach men to seek after Right.[25]

5. O thou the Right, shall I see thee and Good Thought, as one that knows — the throne of the mightiest Ahura and the Obedience of Mazda? Through this word (of promise)[26] on our tongue will we turn the robber horde into the Greatest.

6. Come thou with Good Thought, give through Right, O Mazda, as thy gift to Zarathushtra by thy sure words, long-enduring mighty help, and to us,[27] O Ahura, whereby we may overcome foes.

7. Grant, O thou the Right, the reward, the blessings of Good Thought; O Piety, give our desire to Vishtaspa and to me; O thou, Mazda (Wise one) and Sovereign, grant that your[28] Prophet may perform the word of hearing.

[23] The spirit of animals, or in a wider sense perhaps Nature or the animal world entrusted to man's control.

[24] The souls of his people — collective.

[25] Truth would be nearer here.

[26] *Manthra*, "spell." There seems a conscious transformation of a word hitherto used of mere spells, and destined to revert to this baser use. Zarathushtra's "spells" are promises of heaven, by which he will convert the wild nomads to the Truth.

[27] As in some other places, the Prophet's followers are the speakers, joining him with themselves as a present leader. Zarathushtra might still be the composer, as in verse 7 below.

[28] As often, the plural joins the Amesha with Mazda. Note how the collocation brings out the fact that Mazda is not yet a mere proper name. It would in some ways be more satisfactory to keep "the Wise" throughout, and "Lord" for Ahura.

8. The best I ask of thee, O Best, Ahura (Lord) of one will with the Best Right, desiring them for the hero Frash-aoshtra [29] and myself and for them to whom thou wilt give them, gifts of Good Thought for aye.

9. With these bounties, O Ahura, may we never provoke your wrath, O Mazda, and Right and Best Thought, we who have been eager in bringing you songs of praise. Ye are they that are mightiest to advance desires and the Dominion of Blessings.

10. The wise whom thou knowest as worthy, for their right-doing and their good thought, for them do thou fulfil their longing by attainment. For I know words of prayer are effectual with you, which tend to a good matter.

11. I who would thereby preserve Right and Good Thought for evermore, do thou teach me, O Mazda Ahura, from thy spirit by thy mouth how it will be with the First Life.[30]

### YASNA XXX

1. Now will I proclaim to those who will hear the things that the understanding man should remember, for hymns unto Ahura and prayers to Good Thought; also the felicity that is with the heavenly lights, which through Right shall be beheld by him who wisely thinks.

2. Hear with your ears the best things; look upon them with clear-seeing thought, for decision between the two Beliefs, each man for himself before the Great Consummation, bethinking you that it be accomplished to our pleasure.

3. Now the two primal Spirits, who revealed themselves in vision as Twins, are the Better and the Bad in thought and word and action. And between these two the wise once chose aright, the foolish not so.

4. And when these twain Spirits came together in the be-

---

[29] A noble of the Hvogva family, father-in-law of Zarathushtra and a chief helper.

[30] Life in this world, also called "corporeal life" or "this life," as opposed to "future" or "second" or "spiritual life." He "asks for inspiration that he may set forth the way in which this life may be so lived as to lead on to another."

ginning, they established Life and Not-Life, and that at the last the Worst Existence shall be to the followers of the Lie, but the Best Thought to him that follows Right.

5. Of these twain Spirits he that followed the Lie chose doing the worst things; the holiest Spirit chose Right, he that clothes him with the massy heavens as a garment. So likewise they that are fain to please Ahura Mazda by dutiful actions.

6. Between these twain the demons [31] also chose not aright, for infatuation came upon them as they took counsel together, so that they chose the Worst Thought. Then they rushed together to Violence,[32] that they might enfeeble the world of man.

7. And to him (*i.e.,* mankind) came Dominion, Good Thought and Right; and Piety gave continued life of their bodies [33] and indestructibility, so that by thy retributions through the molten metal [34] he may gain the prize over those others.

8. So when there cometh the punishment of these evil ones, then, O Mazda, at thy command shall Good Thought establish the Dominion in the Consummation, for those who deliver the Lie, O Ahura, into the hands of Right.

9. So may we be those that make this world advance! O Mazda, and ye other Ahuras,[35] gather together the Assembly,

[31] Remembering that the *Daeva* were the old nature-gods, who got their bad character largely through the predatory behavior of their devotees, this verse becomes very suggestive; it preserves the memory of a time when the Daevas had not yet fallen.

[32] *Aesma*, semi-personified here.

[33] Prof. A. V. W. Jackson showed that as Aramaiti is in special charge of the Earth, this involves the idea of a bodily resurrection for those who sleep in her bosom. We might add that it squares badly with the Magian doctrine that the Earth must not receive the bodies of the dead; it presumes burial as practised by the Iranians, and notably by the Achæmenian kings.

[34] *Ayanha*, was expanded into "molten metal." It is the flood which is to be poured out on the Last Day, which will burn up all evil, but leave the good unharmed.

[35] By an idiom frequently paralleled in Aryan, "ye Mazda Ahuras" means "Mazda and the others who bear the title Ahura (Lord)."

and thou too the Right, that thoughts may meet where Wisdom is at home.[36]

10. Then truly on the Lie [37] shall come the destruction of delight; but they that get them good name shall be partakers in the promised reward in the fair abode of Good Thought, of Mazda, and of Right.

11. If, O ye mortals, ye mark those commandments that Mazda hath ordained — of happiness and pain, the long punishment for the liars, and blessings for the righteous — then hereafter shall ye have bliss.

### YASNA XXXII

1. *Zarathushtra.*— And his blessedness, even that of Ahura Mazda, shall the nobles strive to attain, his the community with the brotherhood, his, ye Daeva, in the manner I declare it.

*Representatives of the Classes.*— As thy messengers, we would keep them far away that are enemies to you.

2. To them Mazda Ahura, who is united with Good Thought, and in goodly fellowship with glorious Right, through Dominion, made reply: We make choice of your holy good Piety — it shall be ours.

3. *Zarathushtra.*— But ye, ye Daevas all, and he that highly honors you, are seed of the Bad Thought — yea, and of the Lie and of Arrogance; likewise your deeds, whereby ye have long been known in the seventh region of the earth.[38]

4. For ye have brought it to pass that men who do the worst things shall be called beloved of the Daevas, separating themselves from Good Thought, departing from the will of Mazda Ahura and from Right.

5. Thereby ye defrauded mankind of happy life and of

---

[36] "Wisdom" is really "religion," in the familiar testament sense. The verse becomes a prayer for the speedy coming of the End, when good men's "thoughts" (*mana*) would dwell in "Good Thought" or Paradise, where Religion has her eternal home.

[37] That is, on the followers of the Druj.

[38] The central part of the earth, on which men live.

immortality, by the deed which he [39] and the Bad Spirit together with Bad Thought and Bad Word taught you, ye
Daevas, and the Liars, so as to ruin mankind.

6. The many sins, by which he has attained to be known,
whether by these it shall be thus,[40] this thou knowest by the
Best Thought, O Ahura, who art mindful of man's desert.
In thy Dominion, Mazda, shall your sentence and that of the
Right be passed.

7. None of these sins will the understanding commit, in
eagerness to attain the blessing that shall be proclaimed, we
know, through the glowing metal — sins the issue of which,
O Ahura Mazda, thou knowest best.

8. In these sins, we know, Yima was involved, Vivah-
vant's son, who desiring to satisfy men gave our people flesh
of the ox to eat. From these shall I be separated by thee, O
Mazda, at last.

9. The teacher of evil destroys the lore, he by his teach-
ings destroys the design of life, he prevents the possession of
Good Thought from being prized. These words of my spirit
I wail unto you, O Mazda, and to the Right.

10. He it is that destroys the lore, who declares that the
Ox and the Sun are the worst thing to behold with the
eyes,[41] and hath made the pious into liars, and desolates the
pastures and lifts his weapon against the righteous man.

11. It is they, the liars, who destroy life, who are mightily
determined to deprive matron and master of the enjoyment
of their heritage,[42] in that they would pervert the righteous,
O Mazda, from the Best Thought.

12. Since they by their lore would pervert men from the
best doing, Mazda utters evil against them, who destroy the
life of the Ox with shouts of joy, by whom Grehma and his

[39] It seems that this complex sentence intends to imply that the human
heretic taught the "men of the Druj," and Aka Mainyu taught the
Daevas.

[40] As set forth in verse 5.

[41] According to Bartholomae's convincing exegesis, this points to
nocturnal orgies of daeva-worshipers, associated with slaughter of cattle
and intoxication with *haoma*.

[42] Bartholomae takes this of the heavenly inheritance.

tribe [43] are preferred to the Right, and the Karapan [44] and the lordship of them that seek after the Lie.

13. Since Grehma shall attain the realms in the dwelling of the Worst Thought, he and the destroyers of this life, O Mazda, they shall lament in their longing for the message of thy prophet, who will stay them from beholding of the Right.[45]

14. To his undoing Grehma and the Kavis [46] have long devoted their purposes and energies, for they set themselves to help the liar, and that it may be said " The Ox shall be slain, that it may kindle the Averter of Death [47] to help us."

15. Thereby hath come to ruin the Karapan and the Kavi community, through those whom they will not have to rule over their life. These shall be borne away from them both to the dwelling of Good Thought.

16. . . . ,[48] who hast power, O Mazda Ahura, over him who threatens to be my undoing, that I may fetter the men of the Lie in their violence against my friends.

YASNA XXXIII

1. According as it is with the laws that belong to the present [49] life, so shall the Judge [50] act with most just deed toward the man of the Lie and the man of the Right, and him whose false things and good things balance.

2. Whoso worketh ill for the liar by word or thought or

[43] Literally, " the Grehmas," as we say " the Joneses." This leader of Daeva-worship presides at the orgy.

[44] The name denoted priests of the *daevayasna*.

[45] The beatific vision, for which they will unavailingly long when it is too late.

[46] A name of Iranian chieftains, appropriated (when used separately) to *daevayasna* chiefs; but it had become already attached to the names of a dynasty of Mazdean kings, so that the term retains for Kavi Vishtaspa a good connotation.

[47] *Duraosa* is in Later Avestan the standing epithet of " Haoma," so that we have here a perfectly clear allusion to the old Aryan intoxicant which Zarathushtra banned.

[48] Two words in this line defy all reasonable analysis and appear to be corrupt.

[49] Literally, " former," as often.

[50] The *ratu* is Zarathushtra himself.

hands, or converts his dependent to the good — such men meet the will of Ahura Mazda to his satisfaction.

3. Whoso is most good to the righteous man, be he noble or member of the community or of the brotherhood, Ahura — or with diligence cares for the cattle, he shall be hereafter in the pasture of Right and Good Thought.

4. I who by my worship would keep far from thee, O Mazda, disobedience and Bad Thought, heresy from the nobles, and from the community the Lie that is most near, and from the brotherhood the slanderers, and the worst herdsman from the pasture of the cattle;—

5. I who would invoke thy Obedience as greatest of all at the Consummation, attaining eternal life, and the Dominion of Good Thought, and the straight ways unto Right, wherein Mazda Ahura dwells;

6. I, as a priest, who would learn the straight paths by the Right, would learn by the Best Spirit how to practise husbandry by that thought in which it is thought of: these Twain of thine,[51] O Ahura Mazda, I strive to see and to take counsel with them.

7. Come hither to me, O ye Best Ones, hither, O Mazda, in thine own person and visibly, O Right and Good Thought, that I may be heard beyond the limits of the people. Let the august duties be manifest among us and clearly viewed.

8. Consider ye my matters whereon I am active, O Good Thought, my worship, O Mazda, toward one like you, and, O thou Right, the words of my praise. Grant, O Welfare and Immortality, your own everlasting blessing.

9. That Spirit of thine, Mazda, together with the comfort of the Comrades twain,[52] who advance the Right, let the Best Thought bring through the Reform wrought by me. Sure is the support of those twain, whose souls are one.

10. All the pleasures of life which thou holdest, those that were, that are, and that shall be, O Mazda, according to thy good will apportion them. Through Good Thought advance thou the body, through Dominion and Right at will.

[51] Asha and Vohu Manah.
[52] Welfare and Immortality, who were named in verse 8.

11. The most mighty Ahura Mazda, and Piety, and Right that blesses our substance, and Good Thought and Dominion —harken unto me, be merciful to me, when to each man the Recompense comes.

12. Rise up for me, O Ahura, through Piety give strength, through the holiest Spirit give might, O Mazda, through the good Recompense, through the Right give powerful prowess, through Good Thought give the Reward.

13. To support me, O thou that seest far onward, do ye assure me the incomparable things of your Dominion, O Ahura, as the Destiny of Good Thought. Holy Piety, teach men's Self the Right.

14. As an offering Zarathushtra brings the life of his own body, the choiceness of good thought, action, and speech, unto Mazda, unto the Right, Obedience and Dominion.[53]

### YASNA XXXIV

1. The action, the word, and the worship by which I will give for thee Immortality and Right, O Mazda, and the Dominion of Welfare — through multitudes of these, O Ahura, we would that thou shouldst give them.

2. And all the actions of the good spirit and the holy man, whose soul follows with Right, do ye [54] set with the thought thereof in thine outer court,[55] O Mazda, when ye [54] are adored [56] with hymns of praise.

3. To thee and to Right we will offer the sacrifice [57] with due service, that in thy established Dominion ye may bring all creatures to perfection through Good Thought. For the reward of the wise man is forever secure, O Mazda, among you.[58]

[53] Zarathushtra brings "Dominion" to Mazda by bringing "Obedience."

[54] As elsewhere, the plural includes Mazda and other Ahuras.

[55] The *pairigaetha* is "the place, in later times called the Treasury, where good deeds are stored up until the final Reckoning."

[56] Literally, "at the adoring those of your company."

[57] *Myazda*, an offering of food, as distinguished from *zaothra*, a drink-offering.

[58] Literally, "those like you"— the same word as in verse 2 (note 54).

4. Of thy Fire,[59] O Ahura, that is mighty through Right, promised and powerful, we desire that it may be for the faithful man with manifested delight, but for the enemy with visible torment, according to the pointings of the hand.[60]

5. Have ye Dominion and power, O Mazda, Right and Good Thought, to do as I urge upon you, even to protect your poor man? We have renounced all robber-gangs, both demons and men.

6. If ye are truly thus, O Mazda, Right and Good Thought, then give me this token, even a total reversal of this life,[61] that I may come before you again more joyfully with worship and praise.

7. Can they be true to thee, O Mazda, who by their doctrine turn the known inheritance of Good Thought into misery and woe?[62] I know none other but you, O Right: so do ye protect us.

8. For by these actions they put us in fear, in which peril is for many — in that he the stronger puts in fear me the weaker one — through hatred of thy commandment, O Mazda. They that will not have the Right in their thought, from them shall the Good Thought be far.

9. Those men of evil actions who spurn the holy Piety, precious to thy wise one, O Mazda, through their having no part in Good Thought, from them Right shrinks back far, as from us shrink the wild beasts of prey.

10. The man of understanding has promised to cling to the actions of this Good Thought, and to the holy Piety,

---

[59] The *ayah xsysta*, flood of molten metal.

[60] The Bundahish says, "Afterward they set the righteous man apart from the wicked." The separation (compare the "Bridge of the Separater") is conceived as indicated by motion of the Judge's hand pointing.

[61] That the unseen world would involve a reversal of the conditions of the present is assumed: the sorely tried Prophet asks for some token of divine favor here and now.

[62] *Useuru*, Bartholomae gives up as inexplicable. Geldner made it "energy," others "intelligence," etc. Certainly it is hard to defend it from the suspicion of complete corruption. The whole sentence is doubtful, as the differences of the doctors show.

creator, comrade of Right — wise that he is, and to all the hopes, Ahura, that are in thy Dominion, O Mazda.

11. And both thy gifts shall be for sustenance, even Welfare and Immortality.[63] Piety linked with Right shall advance the Dominion of Good Thought, its [64] permanence and power. By these, O Mazda, dost thou bless the foes of thy foes.

12. What is thine ordinance? What willest thou? what of praise or what of worship? Proclaim it, Mazda, that we may hear what ordinances [65] Destiny will apportion. Teach us by Right the paths of Good Thought that are blessed to go in —

13. Even that way of Good Thought, O Ahura, of which thou didst speak to me, whereon, a way well made by Right, the Selves of the future benefactors shall pass to the reward that was prepared for the wise, of which thou art determinant, O Mazda.

14. That precious reward, then, O Mazda, ye will give by the action of Good Thought to the bodily life of those who are in the community that tends the pregnant cow, the promise of your good doctrine, Ahura, that of the wisdom which exalts communities through Right.

15. O Mazda, make known to me the best teachings and actions, these, O Good Thought, and, O Right, the due of praise. Through your Dominion, O Ahura, assure us that mankind shall be capable according to thy will.

[63] Bartholomae (with the Pahlavi) renders these words here as "ambrosia and nectar," which is likely enough.

[64] Or the "permanence and power" may be that of the beatified: there is no pronoun.

[65] *Razan* here means the final judgment of weal or woe.

# THE GATHAS

## II

## THE GATHA USTAVAITI [1]

YASNA XLIII

1. To each several man, to whom may Mazda Ahura ruling at his will grant after the petitioner's will, I will after his will that he attain permanence and power,[2] lay hold of Right [3] — grant me this, O Piety — the destined gifts of wealth, the life of the Good Thought;

2. And it shall be for him the best [4] of all things. After his longing for bliss may one be given bliss,[5] through thy provident most holy spirit, O Mazda, even the blessings of Good Thought which thou wilt give through Right all the days with joy of enduring life.

3. May he [6] attain to that which is better than good, who would teach us the straight paths to blessedness in this life here of body and in that of thought — true paths that lead to the world where Ahura dwells — a faithful man, well-knowing and holy like thee, O Mazda.[7]

4. Then shall [8] I recognize thee as strong and holy, Mazda,

---

[1] So called from its opening words.

[2] Eternal life and strength in Paradise is meant.

[3] " Right " here means virtually Paradise, as the final abode of the Ideal.

[4] *Vahista* became in Middle Persian the special name for Paradise.

[5] Literally, " good breathing."

[6] The community may be supposed to speak of their Prophet, whether or no he himself is author here. Note that he speaks in the first person till verse 16.

[7] This characteristic division of existence into corporeal and spiritual cuts horizontally the other division into good and evil.

[8] An anticipation of the End introduces a series of visions in which the Prophet has recognized the attributes of Mazda; note the change of tense.

when by the hand in which thou thyself dost hold the destinies that thou wilt assign to the Liar and the Righteous, by
the glow of thy Fire whose power is Right, the might of Good
Thought shall come to me.

5. As the holy one I recognized thee, Mazda Ahura, when
I saw [9] thee in the beginning at the birth of Life, when thou
madest actions and words to have their need — evil for the
evil, a good Destiny for the good — through thy wisdom
when creation shall reach its goal.

6. At which goal thou wilt come with thy holy Spirit, O
Mazda, with Dominion, at the same with Good Thought, by
whose action the settlements will prosper through Right.
Their judgments shall Piety proclaim, even those of thy
wisdom which none can deceive.

7. As the holy one I recognized thee, Mazda Ahura, when
Good Thought came to me and asked me, " Who art thou?
to whom dost thou belong? By what sign wilt thou appoint
the days for questioning about thy possessions and thyself?"

8. Then I said to him: " To the first question, Zarathushtra am I, a true foe to the Liar, to the utmost of my power,
but a powerful support would I be to the Righteous, that I
may attain the future things of the infinite Dominion,
according as I praise and sing [10] thee, Mazda.

9. As the holy one I recognize thee, Mazda Ahura, when
Good Thought came to me. To his question, " For which
wilt thou decide?" I made reply, " At the gift of adoration
to thy Fire, I will bethink me of Right so long as I have
power.

10. " Then show me Right, upon whom I call."

*Mazda.*— " Associating him with Piety, I have come
hither. Ask us now what things we are here for thee to ask.
For thine asking is as that of a mighty one, since he that is
able should make thee as a mighty one possessed of thy
desire."

11. As the holy one I recognized thee, Mazda Ahura, when

[9] " In vision."

[10] *Vaf*, properly to "weave," used of the artistic fitting together of
words. The word is interesting from its suggestion of a poetical
tradition, first cousin to the Vedic.

Good Thought came to me, when first by your words I was instructed. Shall it bring me sorrow among men, my devotion, in doing that which ye tell me is the best?

12. And when thou saidst to me, " To Right shalt thou go for teaching," then thou didst not command what I did not obey: " Speed thee,[11] ere my Obedience [12] come, followed by treasure-laden Destiny, who shall render to men severally the destinies of the twofold award."

13. As the holy one I recognized thee, Mazda Ahura, when Good Thought came to me to learn the state of my desire. Grant it me, that which none may compel you to allow, the wish for long continuance of blessed existence that they say is in thy Dominion.

14. If thy provident aid, such as an understanding man who has the power would give to his friend, comes to me by thy Dominion through Right, then to set myself in opposition against the foes of thy Law, together with all those who are mindful of thy words!

15. As the holy one I recognized thee, Mazda Ahura, when Good Thought came to me, when the still mind taught me to declare what is best: " Let not a man seek again and again to please the Liars, for they make all the righteous enemies."

16. And thus Zarathushtra himself, O Ahura, chooses that spirit of thine that is holiest, Mazda. May Right be embodied, full of life and strength! May Piety abide in the Dominion where the sun shines! May Good Thought give destiny to men according to their works!

### YASNA XLIV

1. This I ask thee, tell me truly, Ahura — as to prayer, how it should be to one of you. O Mazda, might one like thee teach it to his friend such as I am, and through friendly Right give us support, that Good Thought may come unto us.

2. This I ask thee, tell me truly, Ahura — whether at the

[11] To the work of propaganda. Bartholomae observes, " The renovation of mankind must be accomplished speedily, for the beginning of the Second Life is conceived as near at hand."

[12] *Sraosa*, later associated with the Amshaspands. He is an angel of Judgment.

beginning of the Best Existence the recompenses shall bring blessedness to him that meets with them. Surely he, O Right, the holy one, who watches in his spirit the transgression of all, is himself the benefactor unto all that lives, O Mazda.

3. This I ask thee, tell me truly, Ahura. Who is by generation the Father of Right, at the first? Who determined the path of sun and stars? Who is it by whom the moon waxes and wanes again? This, O Mazda, and yet more, I I am fain to know.

4. This I ask thee, tell me truly, Ahura. Who upheld the earth beneath and the firmament from falling? Who the waters and the plants? Who yoked swiftness to winds and clouds? Who is, O Mazda, creator of Good Thought?

5. This I ask thee, tell me truly, Ahura. What artist made light and darkness? [13] What artist made sleep and waking? Who made morning, noon, and night, that call the understanding man to his duty?

6. This I ask thee, tell me truly, Ahura — whether what I shall proclaim is verily the truth. Will Right with its actions give aid at the last? will Piety? Will Good Thought announce from thee the Dominion? For whom hast thou made the pregnant cow [14] that brings good luck?

7. This I ask thee, tell me truly, Ahura. Who created together with Dominion the precious Piety? Who made by wisdom the son obedient to his father? I strive to recognize by these things thee, O Mazda, creator of all things through the holy spirit.

8. This I ask thee, tell me truly, Ahura. I would keep in mind thy design, O Mazda, and understand aright the maxims of life which I ask of Good Thought and Right. How will my soul partake of the good that gives increase?

9. This I ask thee, tell me truly, Ahura — whether for the Self [15] that I would bring to perfection, that of the man

---

[13] This forms a striking contrast to the later Magian dualism.

[14] "In Zarathushtra's teaching the symbol of good fortune."

[15] *Daena.* Bartholomae notes, as important for the connection with the "soul" of verse 8 that *daena* also means "religion," as it does in verse 10.

of insight, the Lord of the Dominion would make me promises of the sure Dominion, one of thy likeness, O Mazda, who dwells in one abode with Good Thought.

10. This I ask thee, tell me truly, Ahura. The Religion which is the best for all that are, which in union with Right should prosper all that is mine, will they duly observe it, the religion of my creed, with the words and action of Piety, in desire for thy future good things, O Mazda?

11. This I ask thee, tell me truly, Ahura — whether Piety will extend to those to whom thy Religion shall be proclaimed? I was ordained at the first by thee: all others I look upon with hatred of spirit.

12. This I ask thee, tell me truly, Ahura. Who among those with whom I would speak is a righteous man, and who a liar? On which side is the enemy? On this, or is he the enemy, the Liar, who opposes thy blessings?[16] How shall it be with him? Is he not to be thought of as an enemy?

13. This I ask thee, tell me truly, Ahura — whether we shall drive the Lie away from us to those who being full of disobedience.will not strive after fellowship with Right, nor trouble themselves with counsel of Good Thought.

14. This I ask thee, tell me truly, Ahura — whether I could put the Lie into the hands of Right, to cast her down by the words of thy lore, to work a mighty destruction among the Liars, to bring torments upon them and enmities, O Mazda.

15. This I ask thee, tell me truly, Ahura — if thou hast power over this to ward it off from me through Right, when the two opposing hosts [17] meet in battle according to those decrees which thou wilt firmly establish. Whether is it of the twain that thou wilt give victory?

16. This I ask thee, tell me truly, Ahura. Who is victorious to protect by thy doctrine all that are? By vision assure me how to set up the judge that heals the world.[18]

[16] Those of future life.

[17] The hosts of Mazdayasnians and Daevayasnians; or perhaps rather the spiritual forces in the great Armageddon that precedes the Renovation.

[18] This seems to be Zarathushtra himself — he is praying for a vision that may openly confirm his designation as a prophet.

Then let him have Obedience coming with Good Thought unto every man whom thou desirest, O Mazda.

17. This I ask thee, tell me truly, Ahura — whether through you I shall attain my goal, O Mazda, even attachment unto you, and that my voice may be effectual, that Welfare and Immortality may be ready to unite according to that promise with him who joins himself with Right.

18. This I ask thee, tell me truly, Ahura — whether I shall indeed, O Right, earn that reward, even ten mares with a stallion and a camel,[19] which was promised to me, O Mazda, as well as through thee the future gift of Welfare and Immortality.

19. This I ask thee, tell me truly, Ahura. He that will not give that reward to him that earns it, even to the man who fulfilling his word gives him what he undertook — what penalty shall come to him for the same at this present? I know that which shall come to him at the last.

20. Have the Daevas ever exercised good dominion? And this I ask of those who see how for the Daevas' sake the *Karapan* and the *Usij* [20] gave the cattle to violence, and how the *Kavi* [20] made them continually to mourn, instead of taking care that they may make the pastures prosper through Right.

### YASNA XLV

1. I will speak forth: hear now and harken now, ye from near and ye from far that desire instruction. Now observe him [21] in your mind, all of you, for he is revealed. Never shall the false Teacher destroy the Second Life,[22] the Liar, in perversion by his tongue unto evil belief.

2. I will speak of the Spirits twain at the first beginning of the world, of whom the holier thus spake to the enemy:

---

[19] It is sufficiently obvious that this is a touch of reality, enough to reduce to absurdity any theory that makes these Gathas move in the sphere of the mystical and the mythical alone.

[20] Priests and Rulers.

[21] The absence of indication who is meant may possibly be put down with the signs that the Gathas have a context that is lost.

[22] The Future Life. It is possible also to render " never again shall he destroy life."

"Neither thought nor teachings nor wills nor beliefs nor words nor deeds nor selves nor souls of us twain agree."

3. I will speak of that which Mazda Ahura, the all-knowing, revealed to me first in this earthly life. Those of you that put not in practise this word as I think and utter it, to them shall be woe at the end of life.

4. I will speak of what is best for this life. Through Right doth Mazda know it, who created the same as father of the active Good Thought, and the daughter thereof is Piety of goodly action. Not to be deceived is the all-seeing Ahura.

5. I will speak of that which the Holiest declared to me as the word that is best for mortals to obey: he, Mazda Ahura, said, "They who at my bidding render him [23] obedience, shall all attain unto Welfare and Immortality by the actions of the Good Spirit."

6. I will speak of him that is greatest of all, praising him, O Right, who is bounteous to all that live. By the holy spirit let Mazda Ahura harken, in whose adoration I have been instructed by Good Thought. By his wisdom let him teach me what is best,

7. Even he whose two awards, whereof he ordains, men shall attain, whoso are living or have been or shall be. In immortality shall the soul of the righteous be joyful, in perpetuity shall be the torments of the Liars. All this doth Mazda Ahura appoint by his Dominion.

8. Him thou shouldst seek to bring to us by praises of worship. "Now have I seen it with mine eye, that which is of the good spirit and of good action and word, knowing by Right Mazda Ahura." May we offer him homage in the House of Song!

9. Him thou shouldst seek to propitiate for us together with Good Thought, who at his will maketh us weal or woe. May Mazda Ahura by his Dominion bring us to work, for prospering our beasts and our men, so that we may through Right have familiarity with Good Thought.

10. Him thou shouldst seek to exalt with prayers of Piety,

[23] Zarathushtra.

him that is called Mazda Ahura [24] forever, for that he hath promised through his own Right and Good Thought that Welfare and Immortality shall be in his Dominion, strength and perpetuity in his house.

11. Whoso therefore in the future lightly esteemeth both the Daevas and those mortals who lightly esteem him [25]— even all others save that one who highly esteemeth him — unto him shall the holy Self of the future deliverer,[26] as Lord of the house, be friend, brother, or father, O Mazda Ahura.

### YASNA XLVI [27]

1. To what land shall I go to flee, whither to flee? From nobles and my peers they sever me, nor are the people [28] pleased with me . . .,[29] nor the Liar rulers of the land. How am I to please thee, Mazda Ahura?

2. I know wherefore I am without success, Mazda: because few cattle are mine, and for that I have but few folk. I cry unto thee, see thou to it, Ahura, granting me support as friend gives to friend. Teach me by the Right the acquisition of Good Thought.

3. When, Mazda, shall the sunrisings come forth for the world's winning of Right, through the powerful teachings of the wisdom of the future Deliverers? Who are they to whose help Good Thought shall come? [30] I have faith that thou wilt thyself fulfil this for me, O Ahura.

4. The Liar stays the supporters of Right from prospering the cattle in district and province, infamous that he is, repellent by his actions. Whoso, Mazda, robs him of dominion or

[24] "Wise Lord"— the title needs translating.

[25] Zarathushtra.

[26] *Saosyant*, that is Zarathushtra himself, in that he believed he would in his own lifetime bring the Renovation.

[27] This is obviously an early Yasna, as the Prophet is still powerless.

[28] These are the three social divisions.

[29] The word *heca* is corrupt and has not been successfully emended. It seems to have disappeared before the Pahlavi translation, in which it is omitted.

[30] Both lines concern the "Future Deliverers," that is, in Zarathushtra's thought, himself and his comrades in the work of the Faith.

of life, he shall go before and prepare the ways of the good belief.[31]

5. If an understanding man should be able to hold one who comes over from his vow and his ties of faith, himself having brought him thereto, and living after the ordinance, a righteous man converting a Liar — then shall he tell it to the nobles, that they may protect him from injury, O Mazda Ahura.

6. But whoso when thus approached should refuse his aid, he shall go to the abodes of the company of the Lie.  For he is himself a Liar who is very good to a Liar, he is a righteous man to whom a righteous man is dear; since thou createdst men's Selves in the beginning, Ahura.

7. Whom, O Mazda, can one appoint as protector for one like me, when the Liar sets himself to injure me, other than thy Fire and thy Thought, through the actions of which twain the Right will come to maturity, O Ahura?  In this lore do thou instruct my very Self.

8. Whoso is minded to injure my possessions, from his actions may no harm come to me!  Back upon himself may they come with hostility, against his own person, all the hostile acts, to keep him far from the Good Life, Mazda, not from the ill!

9. Who is it, a faithful man he, who first taught that we honor thee as mightiest to help, as the holy righteous Lord over action?  What thy Right made known, what the Ox-creator made known to Right, they would fain hear through thy Good Thought.

10. Whoso, man or woman, doeth what thou, Mazda Ahura, knowest as best in life, as destiny for what is Right give him the Dominion through Good Thought.  And those whom I impel to your adoration, with all these will I cross the Bridge of the Separater.[32]

[31] Bartholomae observes that this is a hint to Vishtaspa that he should wage war with the Daevayasnian chiefs. If so, we have presumably passed the point in this certainly composite hymn where the conditions of the opening apply.  There the Prophet is helpless and friendless: the royal convert has not yet been won, as he clearly has been in verse 14.

[32] This Bridge is of very ancient Aryan legend.  At the Day of Judg-

11. By their dominion the Karapans and Kavis accustomed mankind to evil actions, so as to destroy Life. Their own soul and their own self shall torment them when they come where the Bridge of the Separater is, to all time dwellers in the House of the Lie.

12. When among the laudable descendants and posterity of the Turanian Fryana [33] the Right ariseth, through activity of Piety that blesseth substance; then shall Good Thought admit them, and Mazda Ahura give them protection at the Fulfilment.[34]

13. Whoso among mortals has pleased Spitama Zarathushtra by his willingness, a man deserving to have good fame, to him shall Mazda Ahura give Life, to him shall Good Thought increase substance, him we account to be a familiar friend with your Right.

14. *Mazda.*— O Zarathushtra, what righteous man is thy friend for the great covenant? [35]  Who wills to have good fame?

*Zarathushtra.*— It is the Kavi [36] Vishtaspa at the Consummation.[37]  Those whom thou wilt unite in one house with thee, these will I call with words of Good Thought.

15. Ye Haecataspa Spitamas,[38] of you will I declare that

ment all men must cross it to reach Heaven. The unworthy will fall from it into the Hell beneath.

[33] The Turanians became the traditional enemies of Iran. The hostility was one of culture and religion, between Mazda and the Daevas, between agriculturists and nomads. Fryana is proof that individuals might cross over: his clan is heard of in the Later Avesta in terms agreeing with this stanza. Bartholomae calls Tura " an Iranian tribe outside Vishtaspa's dominion, not yet converted, but not hostile to the new faith "— that is, in Gathic times.

[34] The Regeneration.

[35] Apparently a term for the " Bund " of the Zarathushtrian community.

[36] The title has a curious double use, denoting also chiefs of the Daevayasna. We must assume that it got its sinister meaning because Vishtaspa stood alone among princes to whom the title belonged.

[37] As Geldner notes, this dialogue is supposed to take place at the Great Day, when Zarathushtra answers for those with whom he has crossed the Bridge (verse 10).

[38] *Haecat-aspa* was the great-grandfather of Zarathushtra, Spitama a more distant ancestor. Their names here describe a clan of the Prophet's more immediate relatives.

ye can discern [39] the wise and the unwise. . . . Through these actions ye inherit Right according to the primeval laws of Ahura.

16. Frashaoshtra Hvogva,[40] go thou thither with those faithful whom we both [41] desire to be in blessedness, where Right is united with Piety, where the Dominion is in the possession of Good Thought, where Mazda Ahura dwells to give it increase.

17. Where, O Jamaspa Hvogva, I will recount your wrong, not your successes, and with your obedience the prayers of your loyalty, before him who shall separate the wise and the unwise through his prudent counselor the Right, even he, Mazda Ahura.

18. He that holds unto me, to him I myself promise what is best in my possession through the Good Thought, but enmities to him that shall set himself to devise enmity to us, O Mazda and the Right, desiring to satisfy your will. That is the decision of my understanding and thought.

19. He who accomplisheth for me, even Zarathushtra, in accordance with Right that which best agrees with my will, to him as earning the reward of the Other Life shall be that of two pregnant cows, with all things whereon his mind is set. These things wilt thou bring to pass for me who best knowest how, O Mazda.

[39] Or (as Bartholomae), "proclaim to you that ye may discern." The contents of the last line (at ellipsis) may have decided it.

[40] Hvogva is the family name of *Frasa-ustra* and his daughter, whom Zarathushtra married, and of his brother *Jama-aspa* mentioned in verse 17.

[41] Geldner, rightly I think, understands this of Mazda and the Prophet himself, acting as Judge.

# THE GATHAS

## III

## THE GATHA SPENTA-MAINYU

1. By his holy Spirit and by Best Thought, deed, and word, in accordance with Right, Mazda Ahura with Dominion and Piety shall give us Welfare and Immortality.[1]

2. The best work of this most holy Spirit he fulfils with the tongue through the words of Good Thought, with work of his hands through the action of Piety, by virtue of this knowledge; he, even Mazda, is the Father of Right.

3. Thou art the holy Father of this Spirit, which has created for us the luck-bringing cattle, and for its pasture to give it peace has created Piety,[2] when he had taken counsel, O Mazda, with Good Thought.

4. From this Spirit have the Liars fallen away, O Mazda, but not so the Righteous. Whether one is lord of little or of much, he is to show love to the righteous, but be ill unto the Liar.

5. And all the best things which by this holy Spirit thou hast promised to the righteous, O Mazda Ahura, shall the Liar partake of them without thy will, who by his actions is on the side of Ill Thought?

6. Through this holy Spirit, Mazda Ahura, and through the Fire thou wilt give the division of good to the two parties,

---

[1] The stanza is almost a mnemonic, into which with the names of the Amshaspands is woven the triad of Thought, Word, and Deed, as an expansion of "Best Thought." There is much in this hymn to suggest that it was a sort of versified creed for the neophyte, bringing in a maximum of characteristic terms.

[2] Aramaiti is here brought in primarily as Genius of the Earth: Vohu Manah was especially patron of cattle.

with support of Piety and Right. This verily will convert many who are ready to hear.

### YASNA XLVIII

1. When at the Recompensings the Right shall smite the Lie, so that what was long since made known shall be assigned in eternity to Daevas and men, then will it exalt with thy blessings, Ahura, him who prays to thee.

2. Tell me, for thou art he that knows, O Ahura:— shall the Righteous smite the Liar before [3] the retributions come which thou hast conceived? That were indeed a message to bless the world!

3. For him that knows, that is the best of teachings which the beneficent Ahura teaches through the Right, he the holy one, even thyself, O Mazda, that knows the secret lore through the wisdom of Good Thought.

4. Whoso, O Mazda, makes his thought now better, now worse, and likewise his Self by action and by word, and follows his own inclinations, wishes, and choices, he shall in thy purpose be in a separate place at the last.

5. Let good rulers rule us, not evil rulers, with the actions of the Good Lore, O Piety! Perfect thou for man, O thou most good, the future birth, and for the cow skilled husbandry. Let her grow fat for our nourishing!

6. She [4] will give us a peaceful dwelling, she will give lasting life and strength, she the beloved of Good Thought. For it (the cattle) Mazda Ahura made the plants to grow at the birth of the First Life, through Right.

7. Violence must be put down! against cruelty [5] make a stand, ye who would make sure of the reward of the Good Thought through Right, to whose company the holy man

---

[3] The stress is on " before." Zarathushtra is clear about the ultimate victory, but wistfully asks for an earnest of that future.

[4] Armaiti, especially as genius of the Earth. As in Yasna xxx., verse 7 (q.v.), she gives future life: the connection strongly suggests the germs of a doctrine of bodily resurrection.

[5] Aesmo. Both this and remo denote in this context violence and cruelty toward cattle, such as the nomad raiders were constantly showing.

belongs. His dwelling-places shall be in thy House, O Ahura.

8. Is the possession of thy good Dominion, Mazda, is that of thy Destiny [6] assured to me, Ahura? Will thy manifestation,[7] O thou Right, be welcome to the pious, even the weighing of actions by the Good Spirit?

9. When shall I know whether ye have power, O Mazda and Right, over every one whose destructiveness is a menace to me? Let the revelation of Good Thought be confirmed unto me: the future deliverer should know how his own destiny shall be.[8]

10. When, O Mazda, will the nobles understand the Message?[9] When wilt thou smite the filthiness of this intoxicant,[10] through which the Karapans evilly deceive, and the wicked lords of the lands with purpose fell?

11. When, O Mazda, shall Piety come with Right, with Dominion the happy dwelling rich with pasture? Who are they that will make peace with the bloodthirsty Liars? To whom will the Lore of Good Thought come?

12. These shall be the deliverers of the provinces, who follow after pleasing, O Good Thought, by their actions, O Right, depending on thy command, O Mazda. For these are the appointed smiters of Violence.

### YASNA XLIX

1. Ever has Bendva [11] opposed me, my greatest foe, because I desire to win through Right [12] men that are neglected, O Mazda. With the Good Reward come to me, support me, prepare his ruin through Good Thought.

[6] *Asois*, the destined reward.

[7] Apparently the unveiling of all secret things.

[8] A good passage to show what *saosyant* means for Zarathushtra.

[9] The nobles are not yet won over: whether this is before or after Vishtaspa's conversion does not appear.

[10] A very marked allusion to Haoma, who, however, is not named.

[11] A *daevayasna* chieftain. The word means apparently "pestilent"; and Geldner takes it as a title of the evil spirit: on the other view it will be a nickname of the chief.

[12] Or (as Geldner and Bartholomae), "O Right, O Mazda."

2. The perverter [13] of this Bendva has long time impeded me, the Liar who has fallen away from Right. He cares not that holy Piety should be his, nor takes he counsel with Good Thought, O Mazda.

3. And in this belief of ours, O Mazda, Right is laid down, for blessing; in the heresy the Lie, for ruin. Therefore I strive for the fellowship of Good Thought, I forbid all intercourse with the Liar.

4. They who by evil purpose make increase of violence and cruelty with their tongues, the foes of cattle-nurture among its friends; whose ill deeds prevail, not their good deeds: these shall be in the House of the Daevas, the place for the Self of the Liar.

5. But he, O Mazda — happiness and satiety be his who links his own Self with Good Thought, being through Right an intimate of Piety. And with all these may I be in thy Dominion, Ahura.

6. I beseech you twain, O Mazda and the Right, to say what is after the thought of your will, that we may rightly discern how we might teach the Religion that comes from you, O Ahura.

7. And this let Good Thought hear, O Mazda, let the Right hear, do thou thyself listen, O Ahura, what man of the brotherhood, what noble [14] it is according to the law who brings to the community good fame.

8. On Frashaoshtra do thou bestow the most gladsome fellowship with the Right — this I ask of thee, O Mazda Ahura — and on myself the hold on what is good in thy Dominion. To all eternity we would be thy beloved.

9. Let thy helper hear the ordinances, he that is created to bring deliverance. The man of right words is no regarder of fellowship with the Liar, if they that are partakers of Right are to make their Selves partake in the best reward at the Judgment, O Jamaspa.

[13] Bartholomae suggests that this heretic may be the Grehma of whom we hear in Yasna xxxii., verses 12–14.

[14] Bartholomae notes as the meaning that if priests and nobles set a good example, the peasants will also attach themselves to the faith.

10. And this, O Mazda, will I put in thy care within thy House [15]— the Good Thought and the souls of the Righteous, their worship, their Piety and zeal, that thou mayst guard it, O thou of mighty Dominion, with abiding power.

11. But these that are of an evil dominion, of evil deeds, evil words, evil Self, and evil thought, Liars, the Souls [16] go to meet them with foul food: in the House of the Lie they shall be meet inhabitants.

12. What help hast thou, O Right, for Zarathushtra that calls upon thee? what hast thou, Good Thought? — for me who with praises seek your favor, O Mazda Ahura, longing for that which is the best in your possession.

### YASNA L

1. *Zarathushtra.*— Can my soul count on any one for help? Who is there found for my herd, who for myself a protector indeed, at my call other than Right and thyself, O Mazda Ahura, and the Best Thought?

2. How, O Mazda, should one desire the luck-bringing cattle, one who would fain it should come to him together with the pasture?

*Mazda.*— They that live uprightly according to the Right among the many that look upon the sun, these when they stand in the judgment I will settle in the dwellings of the wise.

3. *Zarathushtra.*— So this reward shall come to him through the Right, O Mazda, the reward which by the Dominion and Good Thought he promised, whosoever by the power of his Destiny prospers the neighboring possession that now the Liar holds.

4. I will worship you with praise, O Mazda Ahura, joined with Right and Best Thought and Dominion, that they, desired of pious men, may stand as Judges on the path of the obedient unto the House of Song.

5. Assured by you, O Mazda Ahura and Right, are the

---

[15] The "treasury," as it was afterward called.

[16] Of those "Liars" who have died earlier and preceded them to the hell of which the "foul food" is characteristic.

pointings of the hand — since you are well disposed to your prophet — which shall bring us to bliss, together with visible manifest help.

6. The prophet Zarathushtra, who as thy friend, O Mazda and the Right, lifts up his voice with worship — may the Creator of Wisdom teach me his ordinances through Good Thought, that my tongue may have a pathway.[17]

7. For you I will harness the swiftest steeds, stout and strong, by the prompting of your praise, that ye may come hither, O Mazda, Right and Good Thought. May ye be ready for my help!

8. With verses that are recognized as those of pious zeal I will come before you with outstretched hands, O Mazda, before you, O thou Right, with the worship of the faithful man, before you with all the capacity of Good Thought.

9. With these prayers I would come and praise you, O Mazda and thou Right, with actions of Good Thought. If I be master of my own destiny as I will, then will I take thought for the portion of the wise in the same.

10. Those actions that I shall achieve, and those done aforetime, and those, O Good Thought, that are precious in the sight, the rays of the sun, the bright uprisings of the days, all is for your praise, O thou Right and Mazda Ahura.

11. Your praiser, Mazda, will I declare myself and be, so long, O Right, as I have strength and power. May the Creator of the world accomplish through Good Thoughts its fulfilment of all that most perfectly answers to his will!

[17] May not stray from the right path. Zarathushtra himself is speaking, though he uses the third person in the relative clause.

# THE GATHAS

## IV

## THE GATHA VOHUXSATHRA

1. The good, the precious Dominion, as a most surpassing portion, shall Right achieve for him that with zeal accomplishes what is best through his actions, O Mazda. This will I now work out for us.

2. Before all, O Mazda Ahura, give me the Dominion of your possession, O Right, and what is thine, O Piety. Your Dominion of blessing give through Good Thought to him that prays.

3. Let your ears attend to those who in their deeds and utterances hold to your words, Ahura and Right, to those of Good Thought, for whom thou, Mazda, art the first teacher.

4. Where is the recompense for wrong to be found, where pardon for the same? Where shall they attain the Right? Where is holy Piety, where Best Thought? Thy Dominions, where are they, O Mazda?

5. All this I ask, whether the husbandman shall find cattle in accordance with Right, he that is perfect in actions, a man of understanding, when he prays to him who hath promised unto the upright the true judge,[1] in that he is lord of the two Destinies [2]—

6. Even he, Ahura Mazda, who through his Dominion appoints what is better than good to him that is attentive to his will, but what is worse than evil to him that obeys him not, at the last end of life.

7. Give me, O thou that didst create the Ox and Waters

---

[1] *Ratum:* Zarathushtra means himself.
[2] Heaven and hell. Of course Mazda is the apportioner.

and Plants, Welfare and Immortality,[3] by the Holiest Spirit, O Mazda, strength and continuance through Good Thought at the Judge's sentence.

8. Of those two things will I speak, O Mazda — for one may say a word to the wise — the ill that is threatened to the Liar, and the happiness that clings to the Right. For he the Prophet is glad for him who says this to the wise.

9. What recompense thou wilt give to the two parties by thy red Fire, by the molten Metal, give us a sign of it in our souls — even the bringing of ruin to the Liar, of blessing to the Righteous.

10. Whoso, other than this one,[4] seeks to kill me, Mazda, he is a son[5] of the Lie's creation, ill-willed thus toward all that live. I call the Right to come to me with good destiny.

11. What man is a friend to Spitama Zarathushtra, O Mazda? Who will let himself be counseled by Right? With whom is holy Piety? Or who as an upright man is intent on the covenant of Good Thought?

12. The Kavi's wanton did not please Zarathushtra Spitama at the Winter Gate, in that he stayed him from taking refuge with him, and when there came to him also Zarathushtra's two steeds shivering with cold.

13. Thus the Self of the Liar destroys for himself the assurance of the Right Way; whose soul shall tremble at the Revelation on the Bridge of the Separater, having turned aside with deeds and tongue from the path of Right.

14. The Karapans will not obey the statutes and ordinances concerning husbandry. For the pain they inflict on the cattle, fulfil upon them through their actions and judgments that judgment which at the last shall bring them to the House of the Lie.

15. What meed Zarathushtra hath promised to the men of his covenant, which in the House of Song Ahura Mazda hath

[3] Note the combination with Water and Plants, their province.

[4] Bartholomae suggests that the reference would be made clear by a gesture. If so, it is hardly likely that the evil spirit is intended, as he thinks: rather a human heretic (Geldner), perhaps Grehma.

[5] *Hunus*, curiously specialized in Avestan to denote only "sons" of demoniacal beings.

first attained, for all this I have looked through your blessings, Good Thought, and those of Right.

16. Kavi Vishtaspa hath accepted that creed which the holy Mazda Ahura with Right hath devised, together with the dominion of the Covenant, and the path of Good Thought. So be it accomplished after our desire.

17. The fair form of one that is dear hath Frashaoshtra Hvogva promised unto me: [6] may sovereign Mazda Ahura grant that she attain possession of the Right for her good Self.

18. This creed Jamaspa Hvogva [7] chooses through Right, lordly in substance. This Dominion they choose who have part in Good Thought. This grant me, Ahura, that they may find in thee, Mazda, their protection.

19. This man, O Maidyoimaongha Spitama, [8] hath set this before him after conceiving it in his own Self. He that would see Life indeed, to him will he make known what in actions by Mazda's ordinance is better during this existence.

20. Your blessings shall ye give us, all ye that are one in will, with whom Right, Good Thought, Piety, and Mazda are one, according to promise, giving your aid when worshiped with reverence.

21. By piety the beneficent man benefits the Right through his thinking, his words, his action, his Self. By Good Thought Mazda Ahura will give the Dominion. For this good Destiny I long.

22. He, I ween, that Mazda Ahura knoweth, among all that have been and are, as one to whom in accordance with Right the best portion falls for his prayer, these will I reverence by their names and go before them with honor.

[6] Hvovi, the daughter of Frashaoshtra.

[7] Frashaoshtra's brother, and Zarathushtra's son-in-law.

[8] *Maidyoi-manha*, a cousin of the Prophet, and his earliest convert, according to tradition.

# THE GATHAS

## V

## THE GATHA VAHISTO-ISTI

YASNI LIII

1. *Zarathushtra.*— The best possession known is that of Zarathushtra Spitama, which is that Mazda Ahura will give him through the Right the glories of blessed life unto all time, and likewise to them that practise and learn the words and actions of his Good Religion.

2. Then let them seek the pleasure of Mazda with thought, words, and actions, unto his praise gladly, and seek his worship, even the Kavi Vishtaspa, and Zarathushtra's son [1] the Spitamid, and Frashaoshtra, making straight the paths for the Religion of the future Deliverer which Ahura ordained.

3. Him, O Pourucista,[2] thou scion of Haecataspa and Spitama, youngest of Zarathushtra's daughters, hath Zarathushtra appointed as one to enjoin on thee a fellowship with Good Thought, Right, and Mazda. So take counsel with thine own understanding: with good insight practise the holiest works of Piety.

4. *Jamaspa.*— Earnestly will I lead her to the Faith, that she may serve her father and her husband, the farmers and the nobles, as a righteous woman serving the righteous. The glorious heritage of Good Thought . . .[3] shall Mazda Ahura give to her good Self for all time.

5. *Zarathushtra.*— Teachings address I to maidens marry-

---

[1] *Isat-vastra* by name: it does not happen to occur in the Gathas, which only refer to him here.

[2] *Pourucista* and *Haecataspa* (fourth progenitor of Zarathushtra, in the fifth generation from Spitama).

[3] Here are three corrupt syllables.

ing, and to you bridegrooms, giving counsel. Lay them to heart, and learn to get them within your own Selves in earnest attention to the Life of Good Thought. Let each of you strive to excel the other in the Right, for it will be a prize for that one.

6. So is it in fact, ye men and women! Whatever happiness ye look for in union with the Lie shall be taken away from your person. To them, the Liars, shall be ill food, crying Woe! — bliss shall flee from them that despise righteousness. In such wise do ye destroy for yourselves the spiritual Life.

7. And there shall be for you the reward of this Covenant, if only most faithful zeal be with the wedded pair, that the spirit of the Liar, shrinking and cowering, may fall into perdition in the abyss. Separate ye from the Covenant, so shall your word at the last be Woe!

8. So they whose deeds are evil, let them be the deceived, and let them all howl, abandoned to ruin. Through good rulers let him bring death and bloodshed upon them, and peace from their assaults unto the happy villagers. Grief let him bring on those, he that is Greatest, with the bond of death; and soon let it be!

9. To men of evil creed belongs the place of corruption. They that set themselves to contemn the worthy, despising righteousness, forfeiting their own body — where is the Righteous Lord [4] who shall rob them of life and freedom? Thine, Mazda, is the Dominion, whereby thou canst give to the right-living poor man the better portion.

[4] Here apparently of the human king who executes judgment on earth as Mazda will at the Last Day.

### END OF THE GATHAS

# LATER AVESTAN
## (600–332 B. C.)

# THE ZEND-AVESTA

## THE VENDIDAD

*TRANSLATED BY JAMES DARMESTITIR*

*" While mankind were delivered up to the childish terrors of a future replete with horrors visited upon them from without, the early Iranian sage announced the eternal truth that the rewards of Heaven and the punishments of Hell can only be from within."*

— L. H. MILLS.

*" The Religion of Mazda, O Zarathushtra, cleanses the faithful from every evil thought, word, and deed, as a swift-rushing mighty wind cleanses the plain."*

— VENDIDAD.

# THE VENDIDAD

NEXT to the Gathas the Vendidad is the most important of the Avestan writings. It is the Book of the Law of the modern Parsis, the most venerated of their Scriptures, the most carefully preserved. It belongs, as has been already explained, to what might be called the second cycle of Zoroastrianism, and is certainly not older than 600 B.C. Hence the Vendidad teaches a very different faith from that of the Gathas.

In the Vendidad, myths have clustered around Zoroaster. The Powers of Evil attempt to destroy him in childhood. He has a miraculous combat with Ahriman, the God of Evil. He tells the story of Yima or Gamshid, the Persian Noah. Aside from a few such tales in the opening and closing chapters or " Fargards," the Vendidad is a book of laws, most elaborately detailed, scrupulously analyzed, exactly explained. It is true that the main body of these laws are devoted to matters which will seem trivial to a modern reader; the cow and the dog are given space almost as much as man. Yet there is a real sense and a resolute honesty about the laws which must lead us to respect and admire them. The Zoroastrian faith, even in its Vendidad form, was one for which no modern Aryan need feel ashamed.

It has been argued that by the time of the Vendidad, that is about the time of Cyrus, the Persian faith had become commingled with another, the faith of the Medes as taught by their priesthood, the Magi. The suggestion is at least plausible. Zarathushtra himself knew nothing of this horror of dead bodies — this refusal to bury them in earth, which is almost the main teaching of the Vendidad. In this and in the reverence for fire we have perhaps the chief practical teachings of the intruding Magi. King Cyrus, as we know

from our own Bible, was ready to welcome the gods of every
land.   Under him the Zoroastrian faith could scarcely have
remained the simple religion of its earlier days.   The other
later Avestan books go far beyond the Vendidad in their
search for the miraculous.

# THE VENDIDAD

## FARGARD I.[1]—(THE CREATION)

1. Ahura Mazda spake unto Spitama [2] Zarathushtra, saying:

2. I have made every land dear to its people, even though it had no charms whatever in it: [3] had I not made every land dear to its people, even though it had no charms whatever in it, then the whole living world would have invaded the Airyana Vaego.

3. The first of the good lands and countries which I, Ahura Mazda, created, was the Airyana Vaego,[4] by the Vanguhi

[1] This chapter is an enumeration of sixteen perfect lands created by Ahura Mazda, and of as many plagues created in opposition by Angra Mainyu or Ahriman.

Many attempts have been made, not only to identify these sixteen lands, but also to draw historical conclusions from their order of succession, as representing the actual order of the migrations and settlements of the old Iranian tribes. But there is nothing in the text to support such wide inferences. We have here nothing more than a geographical description of Iran, seen from the religious point of view.

The several plagues created by Angra Mainyu to mar the native perfection of Ahura's creations give instructive information on the religious condition of several of the Iranian countries at the time when this Fargard was written. Harat seems to have been the seat of puritan sects that pushed rigorism to the extreme in the law of purification. Sorcery was prevalent in the basin of the Helmend river, and the Parsis were powerful in Kabul, which is a Zoroastrian way of saying that the Hindu civilization prevailed in those parts, which in fact in the two centuries before and after Christ were known as White India, and remained more Indian than Iranian till the Mussulman conquest.

[2] Or Spitamide. Zarathushtra was descended from Spitama at the fifth generation.

[3] "Every one fancies that the land where he was born and has been brought up is the best and fairest land that I have created."—Commentary.

[4] Airyanem Vaego, Iran-Veg, is the holy land of Zoroastrianism: Zoroaster was born and founded his religion there: the first animal

Daitya.[5]   Thereupon came Angra Mainyu, who is all death, and he counter-created the serpent in the river [6] and Winter, a work of the Daevas.[7]

4. There are ten winter months there, two summer months; and those are cold for the waters, cold for the earth, cold for the trees. Winter falls there, the worst of all plagues.

5. The second of the good lands and countries which I, Ahura Mazda, created, was the plain which the Sughdhas inhabit.[8]

Thereupon came Angra Mainyu, who is all death, and he counter-created the locust,[9] which brings death unto cattle and plants.

6. The third of the good lands and countries which I, Ahura Mazda, created, was the strong, holy Mouru.[10]

Thereupon came Angra Mainyu, who is all death, and he counter-created plunder and sin.[11]

couple appeared there. From its name, "the Iranian seed," it seems to have been considered as the original seat of the Iranian race. It has been generally supposed to belong to Eastern Iran, like the provinces which are enumerated after it, chiefly on account of the name of its river, the Vanguhi Daitya, which was in the Sassanian times (as Veh) the name of the Oxus. But the Bundahish distinctly states that Iran-Veg is "bordering upon Adarbaigan."

[5] The Vanguhi Daitya, belonging to Arran, must be the modern Aras (the classic Araxes).

[6] "There are many *Khrafstras* in the Daitik, as it is said, The Daitik full of *Khrafstras*." Snakes abound on the banks of the Araxes (Morier, "A Second Journey," p. 250) nowadays as much as in the time of Pompeius, to whom they barred the way from Albania to Hyrcania.

[7] Arran (Karabagh) is celebrated for its cold winter as well as for its beauty. At the Nauroz (first day of spring) the fields still lie under the snow. The temperature does not become milder before the second fortnight of April; no flower is seen before May. Summer, which is marked by the migration of the nomads from the plain to the mountains, begins about the 20th of June and ends in the middle of August.

[8] Sogdiana province.

[9] "The plague that fell to that country was the bad locust: it devours the plants and death comes to the cattle."— Gr. Bund.

[10] Margu; Merv.

[11] Doubtful.— The Gr. Bund has: "The plague that fell to that country was the coming and going of troops: for there is always there an evil concourse of horsemen, thieves, robbers, and heretics, who speak untruth and oppress the righteous."— Merv continued to be the resort of Turanian plunderers till the recent Russian annexation.

7. The fourth of the good lands and countries which I, Ahura Mazda, created, was the beautiful Bakhdhi [12] with high-lifted banners.

Thereupon came Angra Mainyu, who is all death, and he counter-created the ants and the ant-hills.

8. The fifth of the good lands and countries which I, Ahura Mazda, created, was Nisaya,[13] that lies between Mouru and Bakhdhi.

Thereupon came Angra Mainyu, who is all death, and he counter-created the sin of unbelief.[14]

9. The sixth of the good lands and countries which I, Ahura Mazda, created, was the house-deserting Haroyu.[15]

Thereupon came Angra Mainyu, who is all death, and he counter-created tears and wailing.[16]

10. The seventh of the good lands and countries which I, Ahura Mazda, created, was Vaekereta,[17] of the evil shadows.

Thereupon came Angra Mainyu, who is all death, and he counter-created the Pairika Knathaiti, who clave unto Keresaspa.[18]

11. The eighth of the good lands and countries which I,

[12] Bakhtri; Balkh.

[13] By contradistinction to other places of the same name. There was a Nisaya, in Media, where Darius put to death the Mage Gaumata.

[14] There are people there "who doubt the existence of God."— Commentary.

[15] Haroyu is modern Herat. "The house-deserting Hare: because there, when a man dies in a house, the people of the house leave it and go. We keep the ordinances for nine days or a month: they leave the house and absent themselves from it for nine days or a month."— Gr. Bund.

[16] "The tears and wailing for the dead," the voceros. The tears shed over a dead man grow to a river that prevents his crossing the Kinvat bridge.—Arda Viraf xvi, 7, 10.

[17] Vaekereta, an older name of Kabul.

[18] The Pairika, in Zoroastrian mythology, symbolizes idolatry. The land of Kabul, till the Mussulman invasion, belonged to the Indian civilization and was mostly of Brahmanical and Buddhistic religion. The Pairika Khnathaiti will be destroyed at the end of the world by Saoshyant, the unborn son of Zarathushtra (when all false religions vanish before the true one; Vd. xix, 5).— Sama Keresaspa, the Garshasp of later tradition, is the type of impious heroism: he let himself be seduced to the Daeva-worship, and Zoroaster saw him punished in hell for his contempt of Zoroastrian observances.

Ahura Mazda, created, was Urva of the rich pastures.[19]

Thereupon came Angra Mainyu, who is all death, and he counter-created the sin of pride.[20]

12. The ninth of the good lands and countries which I, Ahura Mazda, created, was Khnenta which the Vehrkanas [21] inhabit.

Thereupon came Angra Mainyu, who is all death, and he counter-created a sin for which there is no atonement, the unnatural sin.[22]

13. The tenth of the good lands and countries which I, Ahura Mazda, created, was the beautiful Harahvaiti.[23]

Thereupon came Angra Mainyu, who is all death, and he counter-created a sin for which there is no atonement, the burying of the dead.[24]

14. The eleventh of the good lands and countries which I, Ahura Mazda, created, was the bright, glorious Haetumant.[25]

Thereupon came Angra Mainyu, who is all death, and he counter-created the evil work of witchcraft.

15. And this is the sign by which it is known, this is that by which it is seen at once: wheresoever they may go and raise a cry of sorcery, there [26] the worst works of witchcraft

[19] Urva, according to Gr. Bund. Meshan, that is to say, Mesene, the region of lower Euphrates, famous for its fertility: it was for four centuries (from about 150 B.C. to A.D. 225), the seat of a flourishing commercial State.

[20] " The people of Meshan are proud: there are no people worse than they."— Gr. Bund.

[21] " Khnenta is a river in Vehrkana (Hyrcania) ."— Commentary. Consequently the river Gorgan.

[22] See Fargard VIII, 31–32.

[23] Harauvati; corrupted into Ar-rokhag (name of the country in the Arabic literature) and Arghand (in the modern name of the river Arghand-ab).

[24] See Fargard III, 36 *seq.*

[25] The basin of the Erymanthus, now Hermend, Helmend, that is to say, the region of Saistan.

[26] In Haetumant.— " The plague created against Saistan is abundance of witchcraft: and that character appears from this, that all people from that place practise astrology; those wizards produce . . . snow, hail, spiders, and locusts."— Gr. Bund. Saistan, like Kabul, was half Indian, and Brahmans and Buddhists have the credit of being proficient in the darker sciences.

go forth. From there they come to kill and strike at heart, and they bring locusts as many as they want.

16. The twelfth of the good lands and countries which I, Ahura Mazda, created, was Ragha [27] of the three races.[28]

Thereupon came Angra Mainyu, who is all death, and he counter-created the sin of utter unbelief.[29]

17. The thirteenth of the good lands and countries which I, Ahura Mazda, created, was the strong, holy Kakhra.[30]

Thereupon came Angra Mainyu, who is all death, and he counter-created a sin for which there is no atonement, the cooking of corpses.[31]

18. The fourteenth of the good lands and countries which I, Ahura Mazda, created, was the four-cornered Varena,[32] for which was born Thraetaona, who smote Azi Dahaka.

Thereupon came Angra Mainyu, who is all death, and he counter-created abnormal issues in women [33] and barbarian oppression.[34]

19. The fifteenth of the good lands and countries which I, Ahura Mazda, created, was the Seven Rivers.[35]

Thereupon came Angra Mainyu, who is all death, and he counter-created abnormal issues in women and excessive heat.

20. The sixteenth of the good lands and countries which

[27] Ragha, transcribed Rak and identified by the Commentary with Adarbaigan and " according to some " with Rai. There were apparently two Raghas, one in Atropatene, another in Media.

[28] " That means that the three classes, priests, warriors, and husbandmen, were well organized there."— Commentary and Gr. Bund.

[29] " They doubt themselves and cause other people to doubt."— Commentary.

[30] There were two towns of that name (Karkh), one in Khorasan, and the other in Ghaznin.

[31] " Cooking a corpse and eating it. They cook foxes and weasels and eat them."— Gr. Bund. See Fargard VIII, 73–74:

[32] Varn, identified by the Commentary, either with Tabaristan or Gilan. " Four-cornered." Tabaristan has rudely the shape of a quadrilateral.

[33] Fargard XVI, 11 seq.

[34] The aborigines of the Caspian littoral were Anarian savages, the so-called " Demons of Mazana."

[35] Hapta hindava, the basin of the affluents of the Indus, formerly called Hind, by contradistinction to Sindh, the basin of the lower river.

I, Ahura Mazda, created, was the land by the sources of the Rangha,[36] where people live who have no chiefs.[37]

Thereupon came Angra Mainyu, who is all death, and he counter-created Winter,[38] a work of the Daevas.[39]

21. There are still other lands and countries,[40] beautiful and deep, longing and asking for the good, and bright.

## FARGARD II.— (THE FLOOD)[1]

### The Legend of Yima or Gamshed.

### I

1. Zarathushtra asked Ahura Mazda:

O Ahura Mazda, most beneficent Spirit, Maker of the material world, thou Holy One!

[36] The basin of the upper Tigris (Rangha or Arvand, the Tigris).

[37] "People who do not hold the chief for a chief."— Commentary.

[38] The severe winters in the upper valleys of the Tigris.

[39] The Vendidad Sada has here: *taozyaka danheus aiwistara*, which the Gr. Bund. understands as: "and the Tajik (the Arabs) are oppressive there."

[40] "Some say:  Persis."— Commentary.

[1] This Fargard may be divided into two parts.

First part (1–20). Ahura Mazda proposes to Yima, the son of Vivanghat, to receive the law from him and to bring it to men. On his refusal, he bids him keep his creatures and make them prosper. Yima accordingly makes them thrive and increase, keeps death and disease away from them, and three times enlarges the earth, which had become too narrow for its inhabitants.

Second part (21 to the end). On the approach of a dire winter, which is to destroy every living creature, Yima, being advised by Ahura, builds a Vara to keep there the finest representatives of every kind of animals and plants, and they live there a life of perfect happiness.

It is difficult not to acknowledge in the latter legend a Zoroastrian adaptation of the deluge, whether it was borrowed from the Bible or from the Chaldean mythology.  The similitude is so striking that it did not escape the Mussulmans, and Macoudi states that certain authors place the date of the deluge in the time of Gamshed.  There are essential and necessary differences between the two legends, the chief one being that in the monotheistic narration the deluge is sent as a punishment from God, whereas in the dualistic version it is a plague from the Daevas: but the core of the two legends is the same: the hero in both is a righteous man who, forewarned by God, builds a refuge to receive choice specimens of mankind, intended some day to replace an imperfect humanity, destroyed by a universal calamity.

**ZOROASTER.**

*After an ancient rock carving, the only known picture
of Zoroaster.*

Who was the first mortal, before myself, Zarathushtra, with whom thou, Ahura Mazda, didst converse, whom thou didst teach the Religion of Ahura, the Religion of Zarathushtra?

'2. Ahura Mazda answered:

The fair Yima, the good shepherd,[2] O holy Zarathushtra! he was the first mortal before thee, Zarathushtra, with whom I, Ahura Mazda, did converse, whom I taught the Religion of Ahura, the Religion of Zarathushtra.

3. Unto him, O Zarathushtra, I Ahura Mazda, spake, saying: "Well, fair Yima, son of Vivanghat, be thou the preacher and the bearer of my Religion!"

And the fair Yima, O Zarathushtra, replied unto me, saying:

"I was not born, I was not taught to be the preacher and the bearer of thy Religion."

4. Then I, Ahura Mazda, said thus unto him, O Zarathushtra:

"Since thou dost not consent to be the preacher and the bearer of my Religion, then make thou my world increase, make my world grow: consent thou to nourish, to rule, and to watch over my world."

5. And the fair Yima replied unto me, O Zarathushtra, saying:

"Yes! I will make thy world increase, I will make thy world grow. Yes! I will nourish, and rule, and watch over thy world. There shall be, while I am king, neither cold wind nor hot wind, neither disease nor death."

7.[3] Then I, Ahura Mazda, brought two implements unto him: a golden seal and a poniard inlaid with gold.[4] Behold, here Yima bears the royal sway!

8. Thus, under the sway of Yima, three hundred winters

---

[2] "His being a good shepherd means that he held in good condition herds of men and herds of animals."— Commentary.

[3] Section 6 is composed of unconnected Zend quotations, which are no part of the text and are introduced by the commentator for the purpose of showing that "although Yima did not teach the law and train pupils, he was nevertheless a faithful and a holy man, and rendered men holy too."

[4] As the symbol and the instrument of sovereignty.

passed away, and the earth was replenished with flocks and herds, with men and dogs and birds, and with red blazing fires, and there was room no more for flocks, herds, and men.

9. Then I warned the fair Yima, saying: " O fair Yima, son of Vivanghat, the earth has become full of flocks and herds, of men and dogs and birds, and of red blazing fires, and there is room no more for flocks, herds, and men."

10. Then Yima stepped forward, in light,[5] southward,[6] on the way of the sun, and afterward he pressed the earth with the golden seal, and bored it with the poniard, speaking thus:

" O Spenta Armaiti,[7] kindly open asunder and stretch thyself afar, to bear flocks and herds and men."

11. And Yima made the earth grow larger by one-third than it was before, and there came flocks and herds and men, at their will and wish, as many as he wished.

12. Thus, under the sway of Yima, six hundred winters passed away, and the earth was replenished with flocks and herds, with men and dogs and birds and with red blazing fires, and there was room no more for flocks, herds, and men.

13. And I warned the fair Yima, saying: " O fair Yima, son of Vivanghat, the earth has become full of flocks and herds, of men and dogs and birds and of red blazing fires, and there is room no more for flocks, herds, and men."

14. Then Yima stepped forward, in light, southward, on the way of the sun, and afterward he pressed the earth with the golden seal, and bored it with the poniard, speaking thus:

" O Spenta Armaiti, kindly open asunder and stretch thyself afar, to bear flocks and herds and men."

15. And Yima made the earth grow larger by two-thirds than it was before, and there came flocks and herds and men, at their will and wish, as many as he wished.

16. Thus, under the sway of Yima, nine hundred winters passed away, and the earth was replenished with flocks and

[5] That is to say, his body being all resplendent with light.

[6] The warm South is the region of Paradise; the North is the seat of the cold winds, of the demons and hell.

[7] The Genius of the Earth.

herds, with men and dogs and birds, and with red blazing
fires, and there was room no more for flocks, herds, and men.

17. And I warned the fair Yima, saying: " O fair Yima,
son of Vivanghat, the earth has become full of flocks and
herds, of men and dogs and birds, and of red blazing fires,
and there is room no more for flocks, herds, and men."

18. Then Yima stepped forward, in light, southward, on
the way of the sun, and afterward he pressed the earth with
the golden seal, and bored it with the poinard, speaking thus:

" O Spenta Armaiti, kindly open asunder and stretch
thyself afar, to bear flocks and herds and men."

19. And Yima made the earth grow larger by three-thirds
than it was before, and there came flocks and herds and men,
at their will and wish, as many as he wished.

## II

21.[8] The Maker, Ahura Mazda, called together a meeting
of the celestial Yazatas in the Airyana Vaego of high renown,
by the Vanguhi Daitya.[9]

The fair Yima, the good shepherd, called together a meeting of the best of the mortals,[10] in the Airyana Vaego of high
renown, by the Vanguhi Daityu.

To that meeting came Ahura Mazda, in the Airyana Vaego
of high renown, by the Vanguhi Daitya; he came together
with the celestial Yazatas.

To that meeting came the fair Yima, the good shepherd,
in the Airyana Vaego of high renown, by the Vanguhi
Daitya; he came together with the best of the mortals.

22. And Ahura Mazda spake unto Yima, saying:

" O fair Yima, son of Vivanghat! Upon the material
world the evil winters are about to fall, that shall bring the
fierce, deadly frost; upon the material world the evil winters
are about to fall, that shall make snow-flakes fall thick, even
an *aredvi* deep on the highest tops of mountains.

---

[8] Section 20 belongs to the Commentary.

[9] See Fargard I, notes to section 3.

[10] The best types of mankind, chosen to live in the Var and repeople
the earth when the Var opens.

23. " And the beasts that live in the wilderness, and those that live on the tops of the mountains, and those that live in the bosom of the dale shall take shelter in underground abodes.

24. " Before that winter, the country would bear plenty of grass for cattle, before the waters had flooded it. Now after the melting of the snow, O Yima, a place wherein the footprint of a sheep may be seen will be a wonder in the world.

25. " Therefore make thee a Vara, long as a riding-ground on every side of the square,[11] and thither bring the seeds of sheep and oxen, of men, of dogs, of birds, and of red blazing fires.[12]

" Therefore make thee a Vara, long as a riding-ground on every side of the square, to be an abode for men; a Vara, long as a riding-ground on every side of the square, for oxen and sheep.

26. " There thou shalt make waters flow in a bed a *hathra* long; there thou shalt settle birds, on the green that never fades, with food that never fails. There thou shalt establish dwelling-places, consisting of a house with a balcony, a courtyard, and a gallery.

27. " Thither thou shalt bring the seeds of men and women, of the greatest, best, and finest on this earth; thither thou shalt bring the seeds of every kind of cattle, of the greatest, best, and finest on this earth.

28. " Thither thou shalt bring the seeds of every kind of tree, of the highest of size and sweetest of odor on this earth; thither thou shalt bring the seeds of every kind of fruit, the best of savor and sweetest of odor. All those seeds shalt thou bring, two of every kind, to be kept inexhaustible there, so long as those men shall stay in the Vara.

29. " There shall be no humpbacked, none bulged forward there; no impotent, no lunatic; no one malicious, no liar; no one spiteful, none jealous; no one with decayed tooth, no

[11] " Two *hathras* long on every side."— Commentary. A *hathra* is about a mile.

[12] That is to say, specimens of each species.

leprous to be pent up,[13] nor any of the brands wherewith
Angra Mainyu stamps the bodies of mortals.[14]

30. " In the largest part of the place thou shalt make nine
streets, six in the middle part, three in the smallest. To the
streets of the largest part thou shalt bring a thousand seeds
of men and women; to the streets of the middle part, six
hundred; to the streets of the smallest part, three hundred.[15]
That Vara thou shalt seal up with thy golden seal, and thou
shalt make a door, and a window self-shining within."

31. Then Yima said within himself: " How shall I manage to make that Vara which Ahura Mazda has commanded
me to make ? "

And Ahura Mazda said unto Yima: " O fair Yima, son of
Vivanghat! Crush the earth with a stamp of thy heel, and
then knead it with thy hands, as the potter does when
kneading the potter's clay." [16]

32. And Yima did as Ahura Mazda wished; he crushed
the earth with a stamp of his heel, he kneaded it with his
hands, as the potter does when kneading the potter's clay.[17]

33. And Yima made a Vara, long as a riding-ground on
every side of the square. There he brought the seeds of
sheep and oxen, of men, of dogs, of birds, and of red blazing
fires. He made a Vara, long as a riding-ground on every
side of the square, to be an abode for men; a Vara, long as
a riding-ground on every side of the square, for oxen and
sheep.

34. There he made waters flow in a bed a *hathra* long;
there he settled birds, on the green that never fades, with food

[13] " A man, afflicted with leprosy, is not allowed to enter a town and
mix with the other Persians."— Herod. 1, 138. He was supposed to have
sinned against the sun. Ctesias has a tale of how Magabyzes escaped
his enemies by simulating leprosy.

[14] In order that the new mankind may be exempt from all moral and
physical deformities.

[15] This division of the Var into three quarters very likely answers
the distinction of the three classes.

[16] In the Shah Nameh Gamshid teaches the Divs to make and knead
clay " by mixing the earth with water "; and they build palaces at his
bidding. It was his renown, both as a wise king and a great builder,
that caused the Mussulmans to identify him with Solomon.

[17] From the Vendidad Sada.

that never fails.  There he established dwelling-places, consisting of a house with a balcony, a courtyard, and a gallery.

35. There he brought the seeds of men and women, of the greatest, best, and finest on this earth; there he brought the seeds of every kind of cattle, of the greatest, best, and finest on this earth.

36. There he brought the seeds of every kind of tree, of the highest of size and sweetest of odor on this earth; there he brought the seeds of every kind of fruit, the best of savor and sweetest of odor.  All those seeds he brought, two of every kind, to be kept inexhaustible there, so long as those men shall stay in the Vara.

37. And there were no humpbacked, none bulged forward there; no impotent, no lunatic; no one malicious, no liar; no one spiteful, none jealous; no one with decayed tooth, no leprous to be pent up, nor any of the brands wherewith Angra Mainyu stamps the bodies of mortals.

38. In the largest part of the place he made nine streets, six in the middle part, three in the smallest.  To the streets of the largest part he brought a thousand seeds of men and women; to the streets of the middle part, six hundred; to the streets of the smallest part, three hundred.  That Vara he sealed up with the golden ring, and he made a door, and a window self-shining within.

39. O Maker of the material world, thou Holy One! What are the lights that give light in the Vara which Yima made?

40. Ahura Mazda answered: "There are uncreated lights and created lights.[18]  The one thing missed there is the sight of the stars, the moon, and the sun, and a year seems only as a day.

41. "Every fortieth year, to every couple two are born, a male and a female.  And thus it is for every sort of cattle.  And the men in the Vara which Yima made live the happiest life."

42. O Maker of the material world, thou Holy One!

[18] The endless light, which is eternal, and artificial lights.

Who is he who brought the Religion of Mazda into the Vara which Yima made?

Ahura Mazda answered: " It was the bird Karshipta,[19] O holy Zarathushtra! "

43. O Maker of the material world, thou Holy One! Who are the Lord and the Master there?

Ahura Mazda answered: " Urvatad-nara,[20] O Zarathushtra! and thyself, Zarathushtra."

## FARGARD III.— (THE EARTH)[1]

### I

1. O Maker of the material world, thou Holy One! Which is the first place where the Earth [2] feels most happy?

Ahura Mazda answered: " It is the place whereon one of the faithful steps forward, O Spitama Zarathushtra! with the log in his hand,[3] the *Baresma* [4] in his hand, the milk [5] in

---

[19] " The bird Karshipta dwells in the heavens: were he living on the earth, he would be the king of birds. He brought the Religion into the Var of Yima, and recites the Avesta in the language of birds."— Bund. XIX and XXIV.

[20] Zarathushtra had three sons during his lifetime, Isad-vastra, Hvare-kithra, and Urvatad-nara, who were respectively the fathers and chiefs of the three classes, priests, warriors, and husbandmen. Urvatad-nara, as a husbandman, was chosen to be the *ahu* or temperal Lord of the Var, on account of the Var being underground. Zarathushtra, as a heavenly priest, was, by right, the *ratu* or Spiritual Lord in Airyana Vaego, where he founded the Religion by a sacrifice.

[1] The principal subject is, as the Pahlavi book, the Dinkard, has it: What comforts most the Genius of the Earth (Sections 1–6)? What discomforts most the Genius of the Earth (Sections 7–11)? What rejoices the Earth most (Sections 12–35)? In each of these three developments a series of five objects is considered. Series I and II, though expressed in symmetrical terms, do not answer one another: there is greater symmetry, as to the ideas, between the second series and the third. Series I and II are a dry enumeration. The third series contains two interesting digressions, one on the funeral laws, and the other on the sanctity of husbandry.

[2] " The Genius of the Earth."— Commentary.

[3] The wood for the fire-altar.

[4] The *Baresma* (now called *barsom*) is a bundle of sacred twigs which the priest holds in his hand while reciting the prayers. (See Fargard XIX, 18 *seq.* and notes.)

[5] The so-called *giv* or *givam*, one of the elements of the Haoma sacrifice.

his hand, the mortar [6] in his hand, lifting up his voice in good accord with religion, and beseeching Mithra,[7] the lord of the rolling country-side, and Rama Hvastra." [8]

2, 3. O Maker of the material world, thou Holy One! Which is the second place where the Earth feels most happy?

Ahura Mazda answered: " It is the place whereon one of the faithful erects a house with a priest within, with cattle, with a wife, with children, and good herds within; and wherein afterward the cattle continue to thrive, virtue to thrive, fodder to thrive, the dog to thrive, the wife to thrive, the child to thrive, the fire to thrive, and every blessing of life to thrive."

4. O Maker of the material world, thou Holy One! Which is the third place where the Earth feels most happy?

Ahura Mazda answered: " It is the place where one of the faithful sows most corn, grass, and fruit, O Spitama Zarathushtra! where he waters ground that is dry, or drains ground that is too wet." [9]

5. O Maker of the material world, thou Holy One! Which is the fourth place where the Earth feels most happy?

Ahura Mazda answered: " It is the place where there is most increase of flocks and herds."

6. O Maker of the material world, thou Holy One! Which is the fifth place where the Earth feels most happy?

[6] The *Havana* or mortar used in crushing the *Haoma* or *Hom.*

[7] Mithra, the Persian Apollo, sometimes like him identified with the Sun, is invoked here as making the earth fertile. "Why do not you worship the Sun? King Yazdgard asked the Christians. Is he not the god who lights up with his rays all the world, and through whose warmth the food of men and cattle grows ripe?" (Elisaeus.)

[8] The god that gives food its savor: he is an acolyte to Mithra.

[9] Under the Achaemanian kings countrymen who brought water to places naturally dry received the usufruct of the ground for five generations. But for those underground canals (called *Kanats*), which bring water from the mountains all through the Iranian desert, Persia would starve.

Ahura Mazda answered: "It is the place where flocks and herds yield most dung."

## II

7. O Maker of the material world, thou Holy One! Which is the first place where the Earth feels sorest grief?

Ahura Mazda answered: "It is the neck of Arezura,[10] whereon the hosts of fiends rush forth from the burrow of the Druj." [11]

8. O Maker of the material world, thou Holy One! Which is the second place where the Earth feels sorest grief?

Ahura Mazda answered: "It is the place wherein most corpses of dogs and of men lie buried." [12]

9. O Maker of the material world, thou Holy One! Which is the third place where the Earth feels sorest grief?

Ahura Mazda answered: "It is the place whereon stand most of those Dakhmas on which the corpses of men are deposited." [13]

10. O Maker of the material world, thou Holy One! Which is the fourth place where the Earth feels sorest grief?

Ahura Mazda answered: "It is the place wherein are most burrows of the creatures of Angra Mainyu." [14]

11. O Maker of the material world, thou Holy One! Which is the fifth place where the Earth feels sorest grief?

Ahura Mazda answered: "It is the place whereon the wife and children of one of the faithful, O Spitama Zarathushtra! are driven along the way of captivity, the dry, the dusty way, and lift up a voice of wailing."

[10] The neck of Arezura is "a mount at the gate of hell, whence the demons rush forth."—Bund. xii, 8. Arezura was a fiend, son of Ahriman, who was killed by the first man, Gayomard.

[11] Hell, the Druj being assimilated to a burrowing *Khrafstra*. Compare Fargard vii, 24.

[12] "It is declared in the good religion, that, when they conceal a corpse beneath the ground, Spendarmad, the archangel, shudders; it is just as severe as a serpent or scorpion would be to any one in a sleeping-garment, and it is also just like that to the ground."

[13] With regard to Dakhmas, see Fargard vi, 45. "Nor is the Earth happy at that place whereon stands a Dakhma with corpses upon it; for that patch of ground will never be clean again till the day of resurrection.

[14] "Where there are most *Khrafstras*" (noxious animals).

## III

12. O Maker of the material world, thou Holy One. Who is the first that rejoices the Earth with greatest joy?

Ahura Mazda answered: " It is he who digs out of it most corpses of dogs and men."

13. O Maker of the material world, thou Holy One! Who is the second that rejoices the Earth with greatest joy?

Ahura Mazda answered: " It is he who pulls down most of those Dakhmas on which the corpses of men are deposited."

14. Let no man alone by himself [15] carry a corpse. If a man alone by himself carry a corpse, the Nasu [16] rushes upon him, to defile him, from the nose of the dead, from the eye, from the tongue, from the jaws, from the sexual organs, from the hinder parts. This Druj Nasu falls upon him, stains him even to the ends of the nails, and he is unclean, thenceforth, forever and ever.

15. O Maker of the material world, thou Holy One! What shall be the place of that man who has carried a corpse alone?

Ahura Mazda answered: " It shall be the place on this earth wherein are least water and fewest plants, whereof the ground is the cleanest and the driest and the least passed through by flocks and herds, by the fire of Ahura Mazda, by the consecrated bundles of *Baresma,* and by the faithful."

16. O Maker of the material world, thou Holy One! How far from the fire? How far from the water? How far from the consecrated bundles of *Baresma?* How far from the faithful?

17. Ahura Mazda answered: " Thirty paces from the fire,

[15] No ceremony in general can be performed by one man alone. It is never good that the faithful should be alone, as the fiend is always lurking about, ready to take advantage of any moment of inattention. If the faithful be alone, there is no one to make up for any negligence and to prevent mischief arising from it.

[16] The word *Nasu* has two meanings: it means either the corpse or the corpse-demon (the Druj Nasu, that is to say, the demon who takes possession of the dead body and makes his presence felt by the decomposition of the body and infection).

thirty paces from the water, thirty paces from the consecrated bundles of *Baresma,* three paces from the faithful.

18, 19. " There, on that place, shall the worshipers of Mazda erect an enclosure, and therein shall they establish him with food, therein shall they establish him with clothes, with the coarsest food and with the most worn-out clothes. That food he shall live on, those clothes he shall wear, and thus shall they let him live, until he has grown to the age of a *Hana,* or of a *Zaurura,* or of a *Pairista-khshudra.*[17]

20, 21. " And when he has grown to the age of a *Hana,* or of a *Zaurura,* or of a *pairista-khshudra,* then the worshipers of Mazda shall order a man strong, vigorous, and skilful, to cut the head off his neck, in his enclosure on the top of the mountain: and they shall deliver his corpse unto the greediest of the corpse-eating creatures made by the beneficent Spirit, unto the vultures, with these words: ' The man here has repented of all his evil thoughts, words, and deeds. If he has committed any other evil deed, it is remitted by his repentance: if he has committed no other evil deed, he is absolved by his repentance, forever and ever.' "

22. O Maker of the material world, thou Holy One! Who is the third that rejoices the Earth with greatest joy?

Ahura Mazda answered: " It is he who fills up most burrows of the creatures of Angra Mainyu."

23. O Maker of the material world, thou Holy One! Who is the fourth that rejoices the Earth with greatest joy?

Ahura Mazda answered: " It is he who sows most corn, grass, and fruit, O Spitama Zarathushtra! who waters ground that is dry, or drains ground that is too wet.

24. " Unhappy is the land that has long lain unsown with the seed of the sower and wants a good husbandman, like a well-shapen maiden who has long gone childless and wants a good husband.

25. " He who would till the earth, O Spitama Zarathush-

---

[17] *Hana* means, literally, " an old man "; *Zaurura,* " a man broken down by age "; *Pairista-khshudra,* " one whose seed is dried up." These words have acquired the technical meanings of " fifty, sixty, and seventy years old."

tra! with the left arm and the right, with the right arm and the left, unto him will she bring forth plenty of fruit: even as it were a lover sleeping with his bride on her bed; the bride will bring forth children, the earth will bring forth plenty of fruit.

26, 27. "He who would till the earth, O Spitama Zarathushtra! with the left arm and the right, with the right arm and the left, unto him thus says the Earth: 'O thou man! who dost till me with the left arm and the right, with the right arm and the left, here shall I ever go on bearing, bringing forth all manner of food, bringing corn first to thee.'

28, 29. "He who does not till the earth, O Spitama Zara-thushtra! with the left arm and the right, with the right and the left, unto him thus says the Earth: 'O thou man! who dost not till me with the left arm and the right, with the right arm and the left, ever shalt thou stand at the door of the stranger, among those who beg for bread; the refuse and the crumbs of the bread are brought unto thee, brought by those who have profusion of wealth.'"

30. O Maker of the material world, thou Holy One! What is the food that fills the Religion of Mazda?

Ahura Mazda answered: "It is sowing corn again and again, O Spitama Zarathushtra!

31. "He who sows corn sows righteousness: he makes the Religion of Mazda walk, he suckles the Religion of Mazda; as well as he could do with a hundred man's feet, with a thousand woman's breasts, with ten thousand sacrificial formulas.

32. "When barley was created, the Daevas started up; when it grew, then fainted the Daevas' hearts; when the knots came, the Daevas groaned; when the ear came, the Daevas flew away.[18] In that house the Daevas stay, wherein wheat perishes. It is as though red-hot iron were turned about in their throats, when there is plenty of corn.

33. "Then let people learn by heart this holy saying:

[18] The general meaning of the sentence is how the Devs are broken down "by the growing, the increasing, and the ripening of the corn."

' No one who does not eat has strength to do heavy works of
holiness, strength to do works of husbandry, strength to beget
children. By eating every material creature lives, by not
eating it dies away.' "

34. O Maker of the material world, thou Holy One!
Who is the fifth that rejoices the Earth with greatest joy?

Ahura Mazda answered: " It is he who kindly and piously
gives [19] to one of the faithful who tills the earth, O Spitama
Zarathushtra!

35. " He who would not kindly and piously give to one of
the faithful who tills the earth, O Spitama Zarathushtra!
Spenta Armaiti [20] will throw him down into darkness, down
into the world of woe, the world of hell, down into the deep
abyss."

## IV

36. O Maker of the material world, thou Holy One!
If a man shall bury in the earth either the corpse of a dog or
the corpse of a man, and if he shall not disinter it within half
a year, what is the penalty that he shall pay?

Ahura Mazda answered: " Five hundred stripes with the
*Aspahe-astra,* five hundred stripes with the *Sraosho-karana.*"

37. O Maker of the material world, thou Holy One! If
a man shall bury in the earth either the corpse of a dog or the
corpse of a man, and if he shall not disinter it within a year,
what is the penalty that he shall pay?

Ahura Mazda answered: " A thousand stripes with the
*Aspahe-astra,* a thousand stripes with the *Sraosho-karana.*"

38. O Maker of the material world, thou Holy One!
If a man shall bury in the earth either the corpse of a dog
or the corpse of a man, and if he shall not disinter it within
the second year, what is the penalty for it? What is the
atonement for it? What is the cleansing from it?

39. Ahura Mazda answered: " For that deed there is
nothing that can pay, nothing that can atone, nothing that
can cleanse from it; it is a trespass for which there is no
atonement, forever and ever."

[19] The *Asho-dad* or alms. This clause is from the Vendidad Sada.
[20] The Genius of the Earth offended.

40. When is it so?

"It is so, if the sinner be a professor of the Religion of Mazda, or one who has been taught in it.

"But if he be not a professor of the Religion of Mazda, nor one who has been taught in it, then his sin is taken from him, if he makes confession of the Religion of Mazda and resolves never to commit again such forbidden deeds.

41. "The Religion of Mazda indeed, O Spitama Zarathushtra! takes away from him who makes confession of it the bonds of his sin; it takes away the sin of breach of trust; it takes away the sin of murdering one of the faithful; it takes away the sin of burying a corpse; it takes away the sin of deeds for which there is no atonement; it takes away the worst sin of usury; it takes away any sin that may be sinned.

42. "In the same way the Religion of Mazda, O Spitama Zarathushtra! cleanses the faithful from every evil thought, word, and deed, as a swift-rushing mighty wind cleanses the plain.

"So let all the deeds he doeth be henceforth good, O Zarathushtra! a full atonement for his sin is effected by means of the Religion of Mazda."

### FARGARD IV.— (THE LAW)[1]

#### Contracts and Outrages

#### I

1. He that does not restore a loan to the man who lent it steals the thing and robs the man.[2] This he doeth every day, every night, as long as he keep in his house his neighbor's property, as though it were his own.[3]

---

[1] This Fargard is the only one in the Vendidad that deals strictly with legal objects.

[2] "He is a thief when he takes with a view not to restore; he is a robber when, being asked to restore, he answers, I will not."— Commentary.

[3] Every moment that he holds it unlawfully, he steals it anew. "The basest thing with Persians is to lie; the next to it is to be in debt, for this reason among many others, that he who is so must needs sink to lying at last."— Herod. I, 183.

## I a

2. O Maker of the material world, thou Holy One! How many in number are thy contracts, O Ahura Mazda?

Ahura Mazda answered: " They are six in number, O holy Zarathushtra. The first is the word-contract; the second is the hand-contract; the third is the contract to the amount of a sheep; the fourth is the contract to the amount of an ox; the fifth is the contract to the amount of a man; the sixth is the contract to the amount of a field, a field in good land, a fruitful one, in good bearing."

3. The word-contract is fulfilled by words of mouth.

It is canceled by the hand-contract; he shall give as damages the amount of the hand-contract.

4. The hand-contract is canceled by the sheep-contract; he shall give as damages the amount of the sheep-contract.

The sheep-contract is canceled by the ox-contract; he shall give as damages the amount of the ox-contract.

The ox-contract is canceled by the man-contract; he shall give as damages the amount of the man-contract.

The man-contract is canceled by the field-contract; he shall give as damages the amount of the field-contract.

5. O Maker of the material world, thou Holy One! If a man break the word-contract, how many are involved in his sin?

Ahura Mazda answered: " His sin makes his Nabanazdistas [4] answerable for three hundred years." [5]

6. O Maker of the material world, thou Holy One! If a man break the hand-contract, how many are involved in his sin?

Ahura Mazda answered: " His sin makes his Nabanazdistas answerable for six hundred years."

7. O Maker of the material world, thou Holy One! If a

[4] The next of kin to the ninth degree.

[5] See section 11. This passage seems to have puzzled tradition. The Commentary says, " How long, how many years, has one to fear for the breach of a word-contract? — the Nabanazdistas have to fear for three hundred years "; but it does not explain further the nature of that fear; it only tries to reduce the circle of that liability to narrower limits.

man break the sheep-contract, how many are involved in his
sin ?

Ahura Mazda answered: " His sin makes his Nabanazdistas answerable for seven hundred years."

8. O Maker of the material world, thou Holy One. If a
man break the ox-contract, how many are involved in his
sin ?

Ahura Mazda answered: " His sin makes his Nabanazdistas answerable for eight hundred years."

9. O Maker of the material world, thou Holy One! If a
man break the man-contract, how many are involved in his
sin ?

Ahura Mazda answered: " His sin makes his Nabanazdistas answerable for nine hundred years."

10. O Maker of the material world, thou Holy One! If a
man break the field-contract, how many are involved in his
sin ?

Ahura Mazda answered: " His sin makes his Nabanazdistas answerable for a thousand years."

11. O Maker of the material world, thou Holy One! If a
man break the word-contract, what is the penalty that he
shall pay?

Ahura Mazda answered: " Three hundred stripes with
the *Aspahe-astra,* three hundred stripes with the *Sraosho-
karana.*"

12. O Maker of the material world, thou Holy One! If a
man break the hand-contract, what is the penalty that he
shall pay?

Ahura Mazda answered: " Six hundred stripes with the
*Aspahe-astra,* six hundred stripes with the *Sraosho-karana.*"

13. O Maker of the material world, thou Holy One! If a
man break the sheep-contract, what is the penalty that he
shall pay?

Ahura Mazda answered: " Seven hundred stripes with
the *Aspahe-astra,* seven hundred stripes with the *Sraosho-
karana.*"

14. O Maker of the material world, thou Holy One! If a

man break the ox-contract, what is the penalty that he shall pay ?

Ahura Mazda answered: " Eight hundred stripes with the *Aspahe-astra,* eight hundred stripes with the *Sraosho-karana.*"

15. O Maker of the material world, thou Holy One ! If a man break the man-contract, what is the penalty that he shall pay ?

Ahura Mazda answered: " Nine hundred stripes with the *Aspahe-astra,* nine hundred stripes with the *Sraosho-karana.*"

16. O Maker of the material world, thou Holy One ! If a man break the field-contract, what is the penalty that he shall pay ?

Ahura Mazda answered: " A thousand stripes with the *Aspahe-astra,* a thousand stripes with the *Sraosho-karana.*"

## II a

17. If a man rise up with a weapon in his hand, it is an *Agerepta.*[6] If he brandish it, it is an *Avaoirista.* If he actually smite a man with malicious aforethought, it is an *Aredus.* Upon the fifth *Aredus* he becomes a *Peshotanu.*

18. O Maker of the material world, thou Holy One ! He that committeth an *Agerepta,* what penalty shall he pay ?

Ahura Mazda answered: " Five stripes with the *Aspahe-astra,* five stripes with the *Sraosho-karana;*

" On the second *Agerepta,* ten stripes with the *Aspahe-astra,* ten stripes with the *Sraosho-karana;*

" On the third, fifteen stripes with the *Aspahe-astra,* fifteen stripes with the *Sraosho-karana;*

---

[6] In this paragraph are defined the first three of the eight outrages with which the rest of the Fargard deals. Only these three are defined, because they are designated by technical terms. We subjoin the definitions of them found in Sanskrit:

*Agerepta,* " seizing," is when a man seizes a weapon with a view to smite another.

*Avaoirista,* " brandishing," is when a man brandishes a weapon with a view to smite another.

*Aredus* is when a man actually smites another with a weapon, but without wounding him, or inflicts a wound which is healed within three days.

19. " On the fourth, thirty stripes with the *Aspahe-astra*, thirty stripes with the *Sraosho-karana;*

" On the fifth, fifty stripes with the *Aspahe-astra*, fifty stripes with the *Sraosho-karana;*

" On the sixth, sixty stripes with the *Aspahe-astra*, sixty stripes with the *Sraosho-karana;*

" On the seventh, ninety stripes with the *Aspahe-astra*, ninety stripes with the *Sraosho-karana.*"

20. If a man commit an *Agerepta* for the eighth time, without having atoned for the preceding, what penalty shall he pay ?

Ahura Mazda answered: " He is a *Peshotanu:* two hundred stripes with the *Aspahe-astra*, two hundred stripes with the *Sraosho-karana.*"

21. If a man commit an *Agerepta*, and refuse to atone for it, what penalty shall he pay ?

Ahura Mazda answered: " He is a *Peshotanu:* two hundred stripes with the *Aspahe-astra*, two hundred stripes with the *Sraosho-karana.*"

22. O Maker of the material world, thou Holy One! If a man commit an *Avaoirista*, what penalty shall he pay ?

Ahura Mazda answered: " Ten stripes with the *Aspahe-astra*, ten stripes with the *Sraosho-karana;*

" On the second *Avaoirista*, fifteen stripes with the *Aspahe-astra*, fifteen stripes with the *Sraosho-karana.*

23. " On the third, thirty stripes with the *Aspahe-astra*, thirty stripes with the *Sraosho-karana;*

" On the fourth, fifty stripes with the *Aspahe-astra*, fifty stripes with the *Sraosho-karana;*

" On the fifth, seventy stripes with the *Aspahe-astra*, seventy stripes with the *Sraosho-karana;*

" On the sixth, ninety stripes with the *Aspahe-astra*, ninety stripes with the *Sraosho-karana.*"

24. O Maker of the material world, thou Holy One! If a man commit an *Avaoirista* for the seventh time, without having atoned for the preceding, what penalty shall he pay ?

Ahura Mazda answered: " He is a *Peshotanu:* two hundred stripes with the *Aspahe-astra,* two hundred stripes with the *Sraosho-karana."*

25. O Maker of the Material world, thou Holy One! If a man commit an *Avaoirista,* and refuse to atone for it, what penalty shall he pay?

Ahura Mazda answered: "He is a *Peshotanu:* two hundred stripes with the *Aspahe-astra,* two hundred stripes with the *Sraosho-karana."*

26. O Maker of the material world, thou Holy One! If a man commit an *Aredus,* what penalty shall he pay?

Ahura Mazda answered: "Fifteen stripes with the *Aspahe-astra,* fifteen stripes with the *Sraosho-karana.*

27. "On the second *Aredus,* thirty stripes with the *Aspahe-astra,* thirty stripes with the *Sraosho-karana;*

"On the third, fifty stripes with the *Aspahe-astra,* fifty stripes with the *Sraosho-karana;*

"On the fourth, seventy stripes with the *Aspahe-astra,* seventy stripes with the *Sraosho-karana;*

"On the fifth, ninety stripes with the *Aspahe-astra,* ninety stripes with the *Sraosho-karana."*

28. O Maker of the material world, thou Holy One! If a man commit an *Aredus* for the sixth time, without having atoned for the preceding, what penalty shall he pay?

Ahura Mazda answered: "He is a *Peshotanu:* two hundred stripes with the *Aspahe-astra,* two hundred stripes with the *Sraosho-karana."*

29. O Maker of the material world, thou Holy One! If a man commit an *Aredus,* and refuse to atone for it, what penalty shall he pay?

Ahura Mazda answered: "He is a *Peshotanu:* two hundred stripes with the *Aspahe-astra,* two hundred stripes with the *Sraosho-karana."*

30. O Maker of the material world, thou Holy One! If a man smite another and hurt him sorely, what is the penalty that he shall pay?

31. Ahura Mazda answered: "Thirty stripes with the *Aspahe-astra,* thirty stripes with the *Sraosho-karana;*

"The second time, fifty stripes with the *Aspahe-astra,* fifty stripes with the *Sraosho-karana;*

"The third time, seventy stripes with the *Aspahe-astra,* seventy stripes with the *Sraosho-karana;*

"The fourth time, ninety stripes with the *Aspahe-astra,* ninety stripes with the *Sraosho-karana.*"

32. If a man commit that deed for the fifth time, without having atoned for the preceding, what is the penalty that he shall pay?

Ahura Mazda answered: "He is a *Peshotanu:* two hundred stripes with the *Aspahe-astra,* two hundred stripes with the *Sraosho-karana.*"

33. If a man commit that deed and refuse to atone for it, what is the penalty that he shall pay?

Ahura Mazda answered: "He is a *Peshotanu:* two hundred stripes with the *Aspahe-astra,* two hundred stripes with the *Sraosho-karana.*"

34. O Maker of the material world, thou Holy One! If a man smite another so that the blood come, what is the penalty that he shall pay?

Ahura Mazda answered: "Fifty stripes with the *Aspahe-astra,* fifty stripes with the *Sraosho-karana;*

"The second time, seventy stripes with the *Aspahe-astra,* seventy stripes with the *Sraosho-karana;*

"The third time, ninety stripes with the *Aspahe-astra,* ninety stripes with the *Sraosho-karana.*"

35. If he commit that deed for the fourth time, without having atoned for the preceding, what is the penalty that he shall pay?

Ahura Mazda answered: "He is a *Peshotanu:* two hundred stripes with the *Aspahe-astra,* two hundred stripes with the *Sraosho-karana.*"

36. O Maker of the material world, thou Holy One! If a man smite another so that the blood come, and if he refuse to atone for it, what is the penalty that he shall pay?

Ahura Mazda answered: "He is a *Peshotanu:* two hundred stripes with the *Aspahe-astra,* two hundred stripes with the *Sraosho-karana.*"

37. O Maker of the material world, thou Holy One! If
a man smite another so that he break a bone, what is the
penalty that he shall pay?

Ahura Mazda answered: "Seventy stripes with the
*Aspahe-astra,* seventy stripes with the *Sraosho-karana;*

"The second time, ninety stripes with the *Aspahe-astra,*
ninety stripes with the *Sraosho-karana."*

38. If he commit that deed for the third time, without
having atoned for the preceding, what is the penalty that he
shall pay?

Ahura Mazda answered: "He is a *Peshotanu:* two hundred stripes with the *Aspahe-astra,* two hundred stripes with
the *Sraosho-karana."*

39. O Maker of the material world, thou Holy One! If
a man smite another so that he break a bone, and if he refuse
to atone for it, what is the penalty that he shall pay?

Ahura Mazda answered: "He is a *Peshotanu:* two hundred stripes with the *Aspahe-astra,* two hundred stripes with
the *Sraosho-karana."*

40. O Maker of the material world, thou Holy One. If
a man smite another so that he give up the ghost, what is the
penalty that he shall pay?

Ahura Mazda answered: "Ninety stripes with the
*Aspahe-astra,* ninety stripes with the *Sraosho-karana."*

41. If he commit that deed again, without having atoned
for the preceding, what is the penalty that he shall pay?

Ahura Mazda answered: "He is a *Peshotanu:* two hundred stripes with the *Aspahe-astra,* two hundred stripes with
the *Sraosho-karana."*

42. O Maker of the material world, thou Holy One! If
a man smite another so that he give up the ghost, and if he
refuse to atone for it, what is the penalty that he shall pay?

Ahura Mazda answered: "He is a *Peshotanu:* two hundred stripes with the *Aspahe-astra,* two hundred stripes with
the *Sraosho-karana."*

43. And they shall thenceforth in their doings walk after
the way of holiness, after the word of holiness, after the
ordinance of holiness.

## III a [7]

44. If men of the same faith, either friends or brothers, come to an agreement together, that one may obtain from the other, either goods,[8] or a wife,[9] or knowledge, let him who desires goods have them delivered to him; let him who desires a wife receive and wed her; let him who desires knowledge be taught the holy word,

45. during the first part of the day and the last, during the first part of the night and the last, that his mind may be increased in intelligence and wax strong in holiness. So shall he sit up, in devotion and prayers, that he may be increased in intelligence: he shall rest during the middle part of the day, during the middle part of the night, and thus shall he continue until he can say all the words which former *Aethrapaitis* [10] have said.

## IV a

46. Before the boiling water publicly prepared,[11] O Spitama Zarathushtra! let no one make bold to deny having received from his neighbor the ox or the garment in his possession.

## III b

47.[12] Verily I say it unto thee, O Spitama Zarathushtra! the man who has a wife is far above him who lives in continence; he who keeps a house is far above him who has none;

---

[7] We return here to contracts; the logical place of Sections 44–45 would be after Section 16.

[8] The analysis of the Vendidad in the Dinkard has here: "a proof that one professes the Religion well is to grant bountifully to the brethren in the faith any benefit they may ask for."

[9] Woman is an object of contract, like cattle or fields: she is disposed of by contracts of the fifth sort, being more valuable than cattle and less so than fields. She is sold by her father or her guardian, often from the cradle.

[10] A teaching priest.

[11] This clause is intended against false oaths taken in the so-called *Var*-ordeal (see section 54 n.). It ought to be placed before section 49 *bis*, where the penalty for a false oath is given.

[12] Sections 47–49 are a sort of commentary to the beginning of section 44.

he who has children is far above the childless man; [13] he who
has riches is far above him who has none.

48. And of two men, he who fills himself with meat receives in him Vohu Mano [14] much better than he who does
not do so; [15] the latter is all but dead; the former is above
him by the worth of an *Asperena*,[16] by the worth of a sheep,
by the worth of an ox, by the worth of a man.[17]

49. This man can strive against the onsets of Asto-
vidhotu; [18] he can strive against the well-darted arrow; he
can strive against the winter fiend, with thinnest garment
on; he can strive against the wicked tyrant and smite him
on the head; he can strive against the ungodly fasting
Ashemaogha.

## IV b

49 (*bis*). On the very first time when that deed [19] has
been done, without waiting until it is done again,

50. Down there [20] the pain for that deed shall be as hard
as any in this world: even as if one should cut off the limbs
from his perishable body with knives of brass, or still worse;

51. Down there the pain for that deed shall be as hard

[13] "In Persia there are prizes given by the king to those who have
most children."— Herod. I, 136.  "He who has no child, the bridge of
Paradise shall be barred to him.  The first question the angels there will
ask him is, whether he has left in this world a substitute for himself; if
the answer be, No, they will pass by and he will stay at the head of the
bridge, full of grief and sorrow."— Saddar 18.  The primitive meaning
of this belief is explained by Brahmanical doctrine; the man without a
son falls into hell, because there is nobody to pay him the family worship.

[14] Vohu Mano is at the same time the god of good thoughts and the
god of cattle.

[15] "There are people who strive to pass a day without eating, and
who abstain from any meat; we strive too and abstain, namely, from
any sin in deed, thought, or word . . . in other religions, they fast from
bread; in ours, we fast from sin."— Saddar 83.

[16] A *dirhem*.

[17] Or: "is worth an *Asperena*, worth a sheep, worth an ox, worth a
man," which means, according to the Commentary: "deserves the gift
of an *Asperena*, of a sheep's value, an ox's value, a man's value."

[18] Asto-vidhotu, the demon of death (Fargard v, 8).  The man who
eats well has greater vitality.

[19] The taking of a false oath.  Compare section 46.

[20] In hell.

as any in this world: even as if one should nail his perishable body with nails of brass, or still worse;

52. Down there the pain for that deed shall be as hard as any in this world: even as if one should by force throw his perishable body headlong down a precipice a hundred times the height of a man, or still worse;

53. Down there the pain for that deed shall be as hard as any in this world: even as if one should by force impale his perishable body, or still worse;

54. Down there the pain for his deed shall be as hard as any in this world: to wit, the deed of a man, who, knowingly lying, confronts the brimstoned, golden,[21] truth-knowing water with an appeal unto Rashnu [22] and a lie unto Mithra.

55. O Maker of the material world, thou Holy One! He who, knowingly lying, confronts the brimstoned, golden, truth-knowing water with an appeal unto Rashnu and a lie unto Mithra, what is the penalty that he shall pay?

Ahura Mazda answered: "Seven hundred stripes with the *Aspahe-astra*, seven hundred stripes with the *Sraosho-karana.*"

### FARGARD V.— (UNCLEANNESS) [1]

### I a

1. There dies a man in the depths of the vale: a bird takes flight from the top of the mountain down into the depths of the vale, and it feeds on the corpse of the dead man there: then, up it flies from the depths of the vale to the top of the mountain: it flies to some one of the trees there, of the hard-wooded or the soft-wooded, and upon that tree it vomits and deposits dung.

2. Now, lo! here is a man coming up from the depths of

---

[21] The water before which the oath is taken contains some incense, brimstone, and molten gold.

[22] The god of truth.

[1] This chapter and the following ones, to the end of the twelfth, deal chiefly with uncleanness arising from the dead, and the means of removing it from men and things.

the vale to the top of the mountain; he comes to the tree
whereon the bird is sitting; from that tree he intends to take
wood for the fire. He fells the tree, he hews the tree, he
splits it into logs, and then he lights it in the fire, the son
of Ahura Mazda. What is the penalty that he shall pay?

3. Ahura Mazda answered: " There is no sin upon a man
for any Nasu that has been brought by dogs, by birds, by
wolves, by winds, or by flies.

4. " For were there sin upon a man for any Nasu that
might have been brought by dogs, by birds, by wolves, by
winds, or by flies, how soon all this material world of mine
would be only one *Peshotanu*,[2] bent on the destruction of
righteousness, and whose soul will cry and wail![3] so num-
berless are the beings that die upon the face of the earth."

### I b

5. O Maker of the material world, thou Holy One!
Here is a man watering a corn-field. The water streams
down the field; it streams again; it streams a third time;
and the fourth time, a dog, a fox, or a wolf carries some
Nasu into the bed of the stream: what is the penalty that
the man shall pay?

6. Ahura Mazda answered: " There is no sin upon a man
for any Nasu that has been brought by dogs, by birds, by
wolves, by winds, or by flies.

7. " For were there sin upon a man for any Nasu that
might have been brought by dogs, by birds, by wolves, by
winds, or by flies, how soon all this material world of mine
would be only one *Peshotanu,* bent on the destruction of
righteousness, and whose soul will cry and wail! so number-
less are the beings that die upon the face of the earth."

### II a

8. O Maker of the material world, thou Holy One! Does
water kill?[4]

---

[2] " People guilty of death."— Commentary.

[3] After their death, " When the soul, crying and beaten off, is driven
far away from Paradise."— Commentary.

[4] Water and fire belong to the holy part of the world, and come from

Ahura Mazda answered: "Water kills no man: Asto-vidhotu binds him, and, thus bound,[5] Vayu carries him off; and the flood takes him up, the flood takes him down, the flood throws him ashore; then birds feed upon him. When he goes away, it is by the will of Fate he goes."

## II b

9. O Maker of the material world, thou Holy One! Does fire kill?

Ahura Mazda answered: "Fire kills no man: Asto-vidhotu binds him, and, thus bound, Vayu carries him off; and the fire burns up life and limb. When he goes away, it is by the will of Fate he goes."

## III

10. O Maker of the material world, thou Holy One! If the summer is past and the winter has come, what shall the worshipers of Mazda do?

Ahura Mazda answered: "In every house, in every borough, they shall raise three rooms for the dead."

11. O Maker of the material world, thou Holy One! How large shall be those rooms for the dead?

Ahura Mazda answered: "Large enough not to strike the skull of the man, if he should stand erect, or his feet or his hands stretched out: such shall be, according to the law, the rooms for the dead.

12. "And they shall let the lifeless body lie there, for two nights, or for three nights, or a month long, until the birds begin to fly, the plants to grow, the hidden floods to flow, and the wind to dry up the earth.

God: how then is it that they kill? "Let a Gueber light a sacred fire for a hundred years, if he once fall into it, he shall be burned." The answer was that it is not the fire nor the water that kills, but the demon of Death and Fate. "Nothing whatever that I created in the world, said Ormazd, does harm to man; it is the bad Vaî that kills the man." — Gr. Rav. 124.

[5] "Asti-vahat is the bad Vaî who seizes the life of man: when his hand strokes him, it is lethargy; when he casts his shadow upon him, it is fever; when he looks in his eyes, he destroys life and it is called Death."— Bund. XXVIII, 35.

13. "And as soon as the birds begin to fly, the plants to grow, the hidden floods to flow, and the wind to dry up the earth, then the worshipers of Mazda shall lay down the dead on the Dakhma, his eyes toward the sun.

14. "If the worshipers of Mazda have not, within a year, laid down the dead on the Dakhma, his eyes toward the sun, thou shalt prescribe for that trespass the same penalty as for the murder of one of the faithful; until the corpse has been rained on, until the Dakhma has been rained on, until the unclean remains have been rained on, until the birds have eaten up the corpse."

## IV

15. O Maker of the material world, thou Holy One! Is it true that thou, Ahura Mazda, seizest the waters from the sea Vouru-kasha with the wind and the clouds?

16. That thou, Ahura Mazda, takest them down to the corpses?[6] that thou, Ahura Mazda, takest them down to the Dakhmas? that thou, Ahura Mazda, takest them down to the unclean remains? that thou, Ahura Mazda, takest them down to the bones? and that thou, Ahura Mazda, makest them flow back unseen? that thou, Ahura Mazda, makest them flow back to the sea Puitika?

17. Ahura Mazda answered: "It is even so as thou hast said, O righteous Zarathushtra! I, Ahura Mazda, seize the waters from the sea Vouru-kasha with the wind and the clouds.

18. "I, Ahura Mazda, take them down to the corpses; I, Ahura Mazda, take them down to the Dakhmas; I, Ahura Mazda, take them down to the unclean remains; I, Ahura Mazda, take them down to the bones; then I, Ahura Mazda, make them flow back unseen; I, Ahura Mazda, make them flow back to the sea Puitika.

19. "The waters stand there boiling, boiling up in the

6 Zoroaster wonders that Ormazd fears so little to infringe his own laws by defiling waters with the dead. In a Ravaet, he asks him bluntly why he forbids men to take corpses to the water, while he himself sends rain to the Dakhmas.

heart of the sea Puitika, and, when cleansed there, they run
back again from the sea Puitika to the sea Vouru-kasha, toward the well-watered tree, whereon grow the seeds of my
plants of every kind by hundreds, by thousands, by hundreds
of thousands.

20. "Those plants, I, Ahura Mazda, rain down upon the
earth, to bring food to the faithful, and fodder to the beneficent cow; to bring food to my people that they may live on
it, and fodder to the beneficent cow."

## V

21. "This is the best, this is the fairest of all things, even
as thou hast said, O pure Zarathushtra!"

With these words the holy Ahura Mazda rejoiced the holy
Zarathushtra:[7] "Purity is for man, next to life, the greatest good, that purity, O Zarathushtra, that is in the religion
of Mazda for him who cleanses his own self with good
thoughts, words, and deeds."

22. O Maker of the material world, thou Holy One!
This Law, this fiend-destroying Law of Zarathushtra,[8] by
what greatness, goodness, and fairness is it great, good, and
fair above all other utterances?

23. Ahura Mazda answered: "As much above all other
floods as is the sea Vouru-kasha, so much above all other
utterances in greatness, goodness, and fairness is this Law,
this fiend-destroying Law of Zarathushtra.

24. "As much as a great stream flows swifter than a
slender rivulet, so much above all other utterances in greatness, goodness, and fairness is this Law, this fiend-destroying
Law of Zarathushtra.

"As high as the great tree stands above the small plants
it overshadows, so high above all other utterances in greatness, goodness, and fairness is this Law, this fiend-destroying
Law of Zarathushtra.

[7] "When Zoroaster saw that man is able to escape sin by performing
good works, he was filled with joy."— Commentary.

[8] The Law (Datem), that part of the religious system of which the
Vendidad is the specimen, and the object of which is the purification of
man.

25. " As high as heaven is above the earth that it com-
passes around, so high above all other utterances is this Law,
this fiend-destroying Law of Mazda.

" Therefore, he will apply to the Ratu, he will apply to
the *Sraosha-varez;* whether for a *draona*-service [9] that should
have been undertaken and has not been undertaken; or for
a *draona* that should have been offered up and has not been
offered up; or for a *draona* that should have been entrusted
and has not been entrusted.

26. " The Ratu has power to remit him one-third of his
penalty: if he has committed any other evil deed, it is remitted by his repentance; if he has committed no other evil
deed, he is absolved by his repentance forever and ever."

## VI

27. O Maker of the material world, thou Holy One! If
there be a number of men resting in the same place, on the
same carpet, on the same pillows, be there two men near
one another, or five, or fifty, or a hundred, close by one another; and of those people one happens to die; how many of
them does the Druj Nasu [10] envelop with corruption, infection, and pollution?

28. Ahura Mazda answered: " If the dead one be a priest,
the Druj Nasu rushes forth, O Spitama Zarathushtra! she
goes as far as the eleventh and defiles the ten.

" If the dead one be a warrior, the Druj Nasu rushes
forth, O Spitama Zarathushtra; she goes as far as the tenth
and defiles the nine.

" If the dead one be a husbandman, the Druj Nasu rushes
forth, O Spitama Zarathushtra! she goes as far as the ninth
and defiles the eight.

29. " If it be a shepherd's dog, the Druj Nasu rushes
forth, O Spitama Zarathushtra! she goes as far as the eighth
and defiles the seven.

9 The *Srosh-darun*, a service in honor of any of the angels, or of
deceased persons, in which small cakes, called *draona*, are consecrated
in their names, and then given to those present to eat.

10 *Nasu* designates both the corpse and the corpse-demon (the Druj
that produces the corruption and infection of the dead body).

"If it be a house-dog, the Druj Nasu rushes forth, O Spitama Zarathushtra! she goes as far as the seventh and defiles the six.

30. "If it be a *Vohunazga* dog,[11] the Druj Nasu rushes forth, O Spitama Zarathushtra! she goes as far as the sixth and defiles the five.

"If it be a *Tauruna* dog,[12] the Druj Nasu rushes forth, O Spitama Zarathushtra! she goes as far as the fifth and defiles the four.

31. "If it be a porcupine-dog, the Druj Nasu rushes forth, O Spitama Zarathushtra! she goes as far as the fourth and defiles the three.

"If it be a *Gazu* dog, the Druj Nasu rushes forth, O Spitama Zarathushtra! she goes as far as the third and defiles the two.

32. "If it be an *Aiwizu* dog, the Druj Nasu rushes forth, O Spitama Zarathushtra! she goes as far as the second and defiles the next.

"If it be a *Vizu* dog, the Druj Nasu rushes forth, O Spitama Zarathushtra! she goes as far as the next, she defiles the next."

33. O Maker of the material world, thou Holy One! If it be a weasel,[13] how many of the creatures of the good spirit does it directly defile, how many does it indirectly defile?

34. Ahura Mazda answered: "A weasel does neither directly nor indirectly defile any of the creatures of the good spirit, but him who smites and kill it; to him the uncleanness clings forever and ever." [14]

35. O Maker of the material world, thou Holy One! If the dead one be such a wicked, two-footed ruffian, as an ungodly *Ashemaogha*,[15] how many of the creatures of the good

---

[11] A dog without a master.

[12] A hunting dog.

[13] A weasel. The weasel is one of the creatures of Ahura, for "it has been created to fight against the serpent *garza* and the other *khrafstras* that live in holes."— Bund. XIX, 27.

[14] Not that the unclean one can not be cleansed, but that his uncleanness does not pass from him to another.

[15] *Ashemaogha*, a heretic.

spirit does he directly defile, how many does he indirectly defile?

36. Ahura Mazda answered: "No more than a frog does whose venom is dried up, and that has been dead more than a year.[16] Whilst alive, indeed, O Spitama Zarathushtra! such a wicked, two-legged ruffian as an ungodly *Ashemaogha*, directly defiles the creatures of the good spirit, and indirectly defiles them.

37. "Whilst alive he smites the water;[17] whilst alive he blows out the fire;[18] whilst alive he carries off the cow;[19] whilst alive he smites the faithful man with a deadly blow, that parts the soul from the body;[20] not so will he do when dead.

38. "Whilst alive, indeed, O Spitama Zarathushtra! such a wicked, two-legged ruffian as an ungodly *Ashemaogha* robs the faithful man of the full possession of his food, of his clothing, of his wood, of his bed, of his vessels;[21] not so will he do when dead."[22]

## VII

39. O Maker of the material world, thou Holy One! When into our houses here below we have brought the fire, the *Baresma*, the cups, the *Haoma*, and the mortar,[23] O holy Ahura Mazda! if it come to pass that either a dog or a man dies there, what shall the worshipers of Mazda do?

40. Ahura Mazda answered: "Out of the house, O Spitama Zarathushtra! shall they take the fire, the *Baresma*, the

[16] The frog is a creature of Ahriman's, and one of the most hateful. Compare Fargard XIV, 5.

[17] By defiling it, a capital crime.

[18] He extinguishes the Bahram fire, a capital crime.

[19] As a cattle-lifter.

[20] As an assassin.

[21] By defiling them, he deprives the faithful of their use.

[22] "When a wicked man dies, the Druj who was with him during his lifetime seizes him and drags him down to Ahriman; therefore, his body, as the Druj is no longer with it, becomes pure. On the contrary, when it is a righteous man that dies, the Amshaspands take his soul to Ormazd and the Druj settles in the house of the body and makes it impure."— Gujastak Abalish.

[23] In order to perform a sacrifice.

cups, the *Haoma,* and the mortar; they shall take the dead one out to the proper place [24] whereto, according to the law, corpses must be brought, to be devoured there."

41. O Maker of the material world, thou Holy One! When shall they bring back the fire into the house wherein the man has died?

42. Ahura Mazda answered: "They shall wait for nine nights in winter, for a month in summer,[25] and then they shall bring back the fire to the house wherein the man has died."

43. O Maker of the material world, thou Holy One! And if they shall bring back the fire to the house wherein the man has died, within the nine nights, or within the month, what penalty shall they pay?

44. Ahura Mazda answered: "They shall be *Peshotanus:* two hundred stripes with the *Aspahe-astra,* two hundred stripes with the *Sraosho-karana.*"

## VIII

45. O Maker of the material world, thou Holy One! If in the house of a worshiper of Mazda there be a woman with child, and if being a month gone, or two, or three, or four, or five, or six, or seven, or eight, or nine, or ten months gone, she bring forth a still-born child, what shall the worshipers of Mazda do?

46. Ahura Mazda answered: "The place in that Mazdean house whereof the ground is the cleanest and the driest, and the least passed through by flocks and herds, by the fire of Ahura Mazda, by the consecrated bundles of *Baresma,* and by the faithful "—

47. O Maker of the material world, thou Holy One! Haw far from the fire? How far from the water? How far from the consecrated bundles of *Baresma?* How far from the faithful?

48. Ahura Mazda answered: "Thirty paces from the fire; thirty paces from the water; thirty paces from the con-

[24] The Dakhma.
[25] Corruption being worse in summer.

secrated bundles of *Baresma;* three paces from the faithful —

49. "On that place shall the worshipers of Mazda erect an enclosure, and therein shall they establish her with food, therein shall they establish her with clothes."

50. O Maker of the material world, thou Holy One! What is the food that the woman shall first take?

51. Ahura Mazda answered: "*Gomez* mixed with ashes, three draughts of it, or six, or nine, to send down the Dakhma within her womb.

52. "Afterward she may drink boiling milk of mares, cows, sheep, or goats, with pap or without pap; she may take cooked milk without water, meal without water, and wine without water."

53. O Maker of the material world, thou Holy One! How long shall she remain so? How long shall she live thus on milk, meal, and wine?

54. Ahura Mazda answered: "Three nights long shall she remain so; three nights long shall she live thus on milk, meal, and wine. Then, when three nights have passed, she shall wash her body, she shall wash her clothes, with *gomez* and water, by the nine holes, and thus shall she be clean."

55. O Maker of the material world, thou Holy One! How long shall she remain so? How long, after the three nights have gone, shall she sit confined, and live separated from the rest of the worshipers of Mazda, as to her seat, her food, and her clothing?

56. Ahura Mazda answered: "Nine nights long shall she remain so: nine nights long, after the three nights have gone, shall she sit confined, and live separated from the rest of the worshipers of Mazda, as to her seat, her food, and her clothing. Then, when the nine nights have gone, she shall wash her body, and cleanse her clothes with *gomez* and water."

57. O Maker of the material world, thou Holy One! Can those clothes, when once washed and cleansed, ever be used either by a *Zaotar,* or by a *Havanan,* or by an *Atarevakhsha,* or by a *Frabaretar,* or by an *Abered,* or by an

*Asnatar,* or by a *Rathwiskar,* or by a *Sraosha-varez,*[26] or by
any priest, warrior, or husbandman?

58. Ahura Mazda answered: "Never can those clothes,
even when washed and cleansed, be used either by a *Zaotar,*
or by a *Havanan,* or by an *Atare-vakhsha,* or by a *Frabaretar,*
or by an *Abared,* or by an *Asnatar,* or by a *Rathwiskar,* or
by a *Sraosha-varez,* or by any priest, warrior, or husbandman.

59. "But if there be in a Mazdean house a woman who
is in her sickness, or a man who has become unfit for work,
and who must sit in the place of infirmity, those clothes shall
serve for their coverings and for their sheets,[27] until they
can withdraw their hands for prayer.[28]

60. "Ahura Mazda, indeed, does not allow us to waste
anything of value that we may have, not even so much as an
*Asperena's*[29] weight of thread, not even so much as a maid
lets fall in spinning.

61. "Whosoever throws any clothing on a dead body,[30]

[26] These are the names of the different priests who were engaged in
the sacrifices. The *Havanan* strains the *Haoma;* the *Atare-vakhsha*
kindles the fire; the *Frabaretar* brings to the *Zaotar* all that he needs;
the *Abered* brings the water; the *Asnatar* washes and strains the *Haoma;*
the *Rathwiskar* mixes the *Haoma* and the milk; the *Zaotar* chants the
hymns and says the prayers; the *Sraosha-varez* superintends the sacrifice. Nowadays there are only two priests, the *Zaotar* (*Zuti*) and the
*Rathwiskar* (*Raspi*), the latter performing all the accessory services
formerly performed by several priests.

[27] The clothing defiled by the dead can only serve for *Dashtan* women,
even after it has been washed and exposed for six months to the light of
the sun and of the moon.

[28] Until they are clean. The unclean must have their hands wrapped
in an old piece of linen, lest they should touch and defile anything clean.

[29] See Fargard IV, 48, note 16.

[30] Compare Fargard VIII, 23 *seq.* It appears from those passages that
the dead must lie on the mountain naked, or "clothed only with the
light of heaven"—Fargard VI, 51. The modern custom is to clothe
them with old clothing. "When a man dies and receives the order to
depart, the older the shroud they make for him, the better. It must
be old, worn out, but well washed; they must not lay anything new on
the dead. For it is said in the Zend Vendidad, If they put on the dead
even so much as a thread from the distaff more than is necessary, every
thread shall become in the other world a black snake clinging to the
heart of him who made that shroud, and even the dead shall rise
against him and seize him by the skirt, and say, That shroud which

even so much as a maid lets fall in spinning, is not a pious man whilst alive, nor shall he, when dead, have a place in Paradise.

62. "He makes himself a viaticum unto the world of the wicked, into that world,[81] made of darkness, the offspring of darkness, which is Darkness' self. To that world, to the world of Hell, you are delivered by your own doings, by your own religion, O sinners!"

### FARGARD VI.—(UNCLEANNESS)

### I

1. How long shall the piece of ground lie fallow whereon dogs or men have died?

Ahura Mazda answered: "A year long shall the piece of ground lie fallow whereon dogs or men have died, O holy Zarathushtra!

2. "A year long shall no worshiper of Mazda sow or water that piece of ground whereon dogs or men have died; he may sow as he likes the rest of the ground; he may water it as he likes.

3. "If within the year they shall sow or water the piece of ground whereon dogs or men have died, they are guilty of the sin of 'burying the dead' toward the water, toward the earth, and toward the plants."

4. O Maker of the material world, thou Holy One! If worshipers of Mazda shall sow or water, within the year, the piece of ground whereon dogs or men have died, what is the penalty that they shall pay?

5. Ahura Mazda answered: "They are *Peshotanus:* two hundred stripes with the *Aspahe-astra,* two hundred stripes with the *Sraosho-karana.*"

6. O Maker of the material world, thou Holy One! If

thou madest for me has become food for worms and vermin."—Saddar 12. After the fourth day, when the soul is in heaven, then rich garments are offered up to it, which it will wear in its celestial life.—Saddar 87.

[81] "Where darkness can be seized with the hand"; something more than the "visible darkness."

worshipers of Mazda want to till that piece of ground again,[1] to water it, to sow it, and to plow it, what shall they do?

7. Ahura Mazda answered: "They shall look on the ground for any bones, hair, dung, urine, or blood that may be there."

8. O Maker of the material world, thou Holy One! If they shall not look on the ground for any bones, hair, dung, urine, or blood that may be there, what is the penalty that they shall pay?

9. Ahura Mazda answered: "They are *Peshotanus:* two hundred stripes with the *Aspahe-astra,* two hundred stripes with the *Sraosho-karana."*

## II

10. O Maker of the material world, thou Holy One! If a man shall throw on the ground a bone of a dead dog, or of a dead man, as large as the top joint of the little finger, and if grease or marrow flow from it on to the ground, what penalty shall he pay?

11. Ahura Mazda answered: "Thirty stripes with the *Aspahe-astra,* thirty stripes with the *Sraosho-karana."*

12. O Maker of the material world, thou Holy One! If a man shall throw on the ground a bone of a dead dog, or of a dead man, as large as the top joint of the forefinger, and if grease or marrow flow from it on to the ground, what penalty shall he pay?

13. Ahura Mazda answered: "Fifty stripes with the *Aspahe-astra,* fifty stripes with the *Sraosho-karana."*

14. O Maker of the material world, thou Holy One! If a man shall throw on the ground a bone of a dead dog, or of a dead man, as large as the top joint of the middle finger, and if grease or marrow flow from it on to the ground, what penalty shall he pay?

15. Ahura Mazda answered: "Seventy stripes with the *Aspahe-astra,* seventy stripes with the *Sraosho-karana."*

16. O Maker of the material world, thou Holy One! If a man shall throw on the ground a bone of a dead dog, or

[1] Even when a year's space is past, the ground is not free *ipso facto.*

of a dead man, as large as a finger or as a rib, and if grease or marrow flow from it on to the ground, what penalty shall he pay?

17. Ahura Mazda answered: "Ninety stripes with the *Aspahe-astra*, ninety stripes with the *Sraosho-karana*."

[The remainder of this Fargard and the Fargards that come next continue in similar extended detail, each law dealing with the corruption that comes after death, the methods and the spells by which it must be avoided. Not until the thirteenth Fargard does the subject change. Therefore we pass here at once to the twelfth as closing the Fargards upon death.]

FARGARD XII.— (THE MOURNING)[1]

1. If one's father or mother dies, how long shall they stay in mourning, the son for his father, the daughter for her mother? How long for the righteous? How long for the sinners?[2]

Ahura Mazda answered: "They shall stay thirty days for the righteous, sixty days for the sinners."

2. O Maker of the material world, thou Holy One! How shall I cleanse the house? How shall it be clean again?

Ahura Mazda answered: "You shall wash your bodies three times, you shall wash your clothes three times, you shall chant the Gathas three times; you shall offer up a sacrifice to my Fire, you shall bind the bundles of *Baresma*, you shall bring libations to the good waters;[3] then the house shall be clean, and then the waters may enter, then the fire may enter,

[1] The directions in this Fargard are of a special character, and apply only to the near relatives of the dead. Their object is to determine how long the time of "staying" (*upaman*) should last for different relatives. What is meant by this word is not explained; but, as the word *upaman* is usually employed to indicate the staying of the unclean in the *Armest-gah*, apart from the faithful and from every clean object, that word *upaman* seems to show a certain period of mourning, marked by abstention from usual avocations.

The length of the *upaman* varies with the degrees of relationship; and at every degree it is double for relations who have died in a state of sin.

[2] How long if the dead person died in a state of holiness (a *dakma*)? How long if in the state of a *Peshotanu*?

[3] This refers probably to the sacrifice that is offered on each of the

and then the Amesha-Spentas may enter,[4] O Spitama Zara-thushtra!"

3. If one's son or daughter dies, how long shall they stay, the father for his son, the mother for her daughter? How long for the righteous? How long for the sinners?

Ahura Mazda answered: "They shall stay thirty days for the righteous, sixty days for the sinners."

4. O Maker of the material world, thou Holy One! How shall I cleanse the house? How shall it be clean again?

Ahura Mazda answered: "You shall wash your bodies three times, you shall wash your clothes three times, you shall chant the Gathas three times; you shall offer up a sac-rifice to my Fire, you shall bind up the bundles of *Baresma,* you shall bring libations to the good waters; then the house shall be clean, and then the waters may enter, then the fire may enter, and then the Amesha-Spentas may enter, O Spi-tama Zarathushtra!"

5. If one's brother or sister dies, how long shall they stay, the brother for his brother, the sister for her sister? How long for the righteous? How long for the sinners?

Ahura Mazda answered: "They shall stay thirty days for the righteous, sixty days for the sinners."

6. O Maker of the material world, thou Holy One! How shall I cleanse the house? How shall it be clean again?

Ahura Mazda answered: "You shall wash your bodies three times, you shall wash your clothes three times, you shall chant the Gathas three times; you shall offer up a sac-rifice to my Fire, you shall bind up the bundles of *Baresma,* you shall bring libations to the good waters; then the house shall be clean, and then the waters may enter, then the fire may enter, and then the Amesha-Spentas may enter, O Spi-tama Zarathushtra!"

7. If the master of the house[5] dies, or if the mistress of

three days that follow the death of a Zoroastrian for the salvation of his soul.

[4] All the other objects over which the Amesha-Spentas preside (such as the cow, the metals, etc.).

[5] The chief of the family, the *paterfamilias.* The Zoroastrian family is organized on the patriarchal system.

the house dies, how long shall they stay? How long for the righteous? How long for the sinners?

Ahura Mazda answered: "They [6] shall stay six months for the righteous, a year for the sinners."

8. O Maker of the material world, thou Holy One! How shall I cleanse the house? How shall it be clean again?

Ahura Mazda answered: "You shall wash your bodies three times, you shall wash your clothes three times, you shall chant the Gathas three times; you shall offer up a sacrifice to my Fire, you shall bind up the bundles of *Baresma,* you shall bring libations to the good waters; then the house shall be clean, and then the waters may enter, then the fire may enter, and then the Amesha-Spentas may enter, O Spitama Zarathushtra!"

9. If one's grandfather or grandmother dies, how long shall they stay, the grandson for his grandfather, the granddaughter for her grandmother? How long for the righteous? How long for the sinners?

Ahura Mazda answered: "They shall stay twenty-five days for the righteous, fifty days for the sinners."

10. O Maker of the material world, thou Holy One! How shall I cleanse the house? How shall it be clean again?

Ahura Mazda answered: "You shall wash your bodies three times, you shall wash your clothes three times, you shall chant the Gathas three times; you shall offer up a sacrifice to my Fire, you shall bind up the bundles of *Baresma,* you shall bring libations to the good waters; then the house shall be clean, and then the waters may enter, then the fire may enter, and then the Amesha-Spentas may enter, O Spitama Zarathushtra!"

11. If one's grandson or granddaughter dies, how long shall they stay, the grandfather for his grandson, the grandmother for her granddaughter? How long for the righteous? How long for the sinners?

Ahura Mazda answered: "They shall stay twenty-five days for the righteous, fifty days for the sinners."

12. O Maker of the material world, thou Holy One!

[6] All the *familia,* both relatives and servants.

How shall I cleanse the house? How shall it be clean again?

Ahura Mazda answered: " You shall wash your bodies three times, you shall wash your clothes three times, you shall chant the Gathas three times; you shall offer up a sacrifice to my Fire, you shall bind up the bundles of *Baresma,* you shall bring libations to the good waters; then the house shall be clean, and then the waters may enter, then the fire may enter, and then the Amesha-Spentas may enter, O Spitama Zarathushtra!"

13. If one's uncle or aunt dies, how long shall they stay, the nephew for his uncle, the niece for her aunt? How long for the righteous? How long for the sinners?

Ahura Mazda answered: "They shall stay twenty days for the righteous, forty days for the sinners."

14. O Maker of the material world, thou Holy One! How shall I cleanse the house? How shall it be clean again?

Ahura Mazda answered: "You shall wash your bodies three times, you shall wash your clothes three times, you shall chant the Gathas three times; you shall offer up a sacrifice to my Fire, you shall bind up the bundles of *Baresma,* you shall bring libations to the good waters; then the house shall be clean, and then the waters may enter, then the fire may enter, and then the Amesha-Spentas may enter, O Spitama Zarathushtra!"

15. If one's male cousin or female cousin dies how long shall they stay? How long for the righteous? How long for the sinners?

Ahura Mazda answered: "They shall stay fifteen days for the righteous, thirty days for the sinners."

16. O Maker of the material world, thou Holy One! How shall I cleanse the house? How shall it be clean again?

Ahura Mazda answered: "You shall wash your bodies three times, you shall wash your clothes three times, you shall chant the Gathas three times; you shall offer up a sacrifice to my Fire, you shall bind up the bundles of *Baresma,* you shall bring libations to the good waters; then the house shall be clean, and then the waters may enter, then the fire may enter, and then the Amesha-Spentas may enter, O Spitama Zarathushtra! "

17. If the son or the daughter of a cousin dies, how long shall they stay? How long for the righteous? How long for the sinners?

Ahura Mazda answered: "They shall stay ten days for the righteous, twenty days for the sinners."

18. O Maker of the material world, thou Holy One! How shall I cleanse the house? How shall it be clean again?

Ahura Mazda answered: "You shall wash your bodies three times, you shall wash your clothes three times, you shall chant the Gathas three times; you shall offer up a sacrifice to my Fire, you shall bind up the bundles of *Baresma,* you shall bring libations to the good waters; then the house shall be clean, and then the waters may enter, then the fire may enter, and then the Amesha-Spentas may enter, O Spitama Zarathushtra! "

19. If the grandson of a cousin or the granddaughter of a cousin dies, how long shall they stay? How long for the righteous? How long for the sinners?

Ahura Mazda answered: "They shall stay five days for the righteous, ten days for the sinners."

20. O Maker of the material world, thou Holy One! How shall I cleanse the house? How shall it be clean again?

Ahura Mazda answered: "You shall wash your bodies three times, you shall wash your clothes three times, you shall chant the Gathas three times; you shall offer up a sacrifice to my Fire, you shall bind up the bundles of *Baresma,* you shall bring libations to the good waters; then the house shall be clean, and then the waters may enter, then the fire may enter, and then the Amesha-Spentas may enter, O Spitama Zarathushtra! "

21. If a man dies, of whatever race he is, who does not belong to the true faith, or the true law,[7] what part of the creation of the good spirit does he directly defile? What part does he indirectly defile?

---

[7] An infidel, whether he is a relation or not.

22. Ahura Mazda answered: "No more than a frog does whose venom is dried up, and that has been dead more than a year. Whilst alive, indeed, O Spitama Zarathushtra! such wicked, two-legged ruffian as an ungodly *Ashemaogha,* directly defiles the creatures of the Good Spirit, and indirectly defiles them.

23. "Whilst alive he smites the water; whilst alive he blows out the fire; whilst alive he carries off the cow; whilst alive he smites the faithful man with a deadly blow, that parts the soul from the body; not so will he do when dead.

24. "Whilst alive, indeed, O Spitama Zarathushtra! such wicked, two-legged ruffian as an ungodly *Ashemaogha,* robs the faithful man of the full possession of his food, of his clothing, of his wood, of his bed, of his vessels; not so will he do when dead."

### FARGARD XIII.— (THE DOG.) [1]

### I a

1. Which is the good creature among the creatures of the Good Spirit that from midnight till the sun is up goes and kills thousands of the creatures of the Evil Spirit?

2. Ahura Mazda answered: "The dog with the prickly back, with the long and thin muzzle, the dog *Vanghapara,*[2] which evil-speaking people call the *Duzaka;*[3] this is the good creature among the creatures of the Good Spirit that from midnight till the sun is up goes and kills thousands of the creatures of the Evil Spirit.

[1] This Fargard is the only complete fragment, still in existence, of a large canine literature: a whole section of the Ganba-sar-nigat Nask was dedicated to the dog.

[2] The hedgehog. "The hedgehog, according to the Bund. xix, 28, is created in opposition to the ant that carries off grain, as it says that the hedgehog, every time that it voids urine into an ants' nest, will destroy a thousand ants."— Bund. xix, 28. When the Arabs conquered Saistan, the inhabitants submitted on the condition that hedgehogs should not be killed nor hunted for, as they got rid of the vipers which swarm in that country. Every house had its hedgehog. Plutarch counts the hedgehog amongst the animals sacred to the Magi.

[3] *Duzaka* is the popular name of the hedgehog (Persian, *suza*). It is not without importance which name is given to a being: "When called by its high name, it is powerful."— Commentary.

3. "And whosoever, O Zarathushtra, shall kill the dog with the prickly back, with the long and thin muzzle, the dog *Vanghapara,* which evil-speaking people call the *Duzaka,* kills his own soul for nine generations, nor shall he find a way over the Kinvad bridge,[4] unless he has, while alive, atoned for his sin."

4. O Maker of the material world, thou Holy One! If a man kill the dog with the prickly back, with the long and thin muzzle, the dog *Vanghapara,* which evil-speaking people call the *Duzaka,* what is the penalty that he shall pay?

Ahura Mazda answered: "A thousand stripes with the *Aspahe-astra,* a thousand stripes with the *Sraosho-karana.*"

### I b

5. Which is the evil creature among the creatures of the Evil Spirit that from midnight till the sun is up goes and kills thousands of the creatures of the Good Spirit?

6. Ahura Mazda answered: "The daeva *Zairimyangura,*[5] which evil-speaking people call the *Zairimyaka,* this is the evil creature among the creatures of the Evil Spirit that from midnight till the sun is up goes and kills thousands of the creatures of the Good Spirit.

7. "And whosoever, O Zarathushtra! shall kill the daeva *Zairimyangura,* which evil-speaking people call the *Zairim-yaka,* his sins in thought, word, and deed are redeemed as they would be by a Patet; his sins in thought, word, and deed are atoned for.

### II

8. "Whosoever shall smite either a shepherd's dog, or a house-dog, or a *Vohunazga* dog, or a trained dog, his soul when passing to the other world, shall fly howling louder and more sorely grieved than the sheep does in the lofty forest where the wolf ranges.

9. "No soul will come and meet his departing soul and help it, howling and grieved in the other world; nor will the

[4] The bridge leading to Paradise.
[5] The tortoise.

dogs that keep the Kinvad bridge help his departing soul howling and grieved in the other world.

10. "If a man shall smite a shepherd's dog so that it becomes unfit for work, if he shall cut off its ear or its paw, and thereupon a thief or a wolf break in and carry away sheep from the fold, without the dog giving any warning, the man shall pay for the loss, and he shall pay for the wound of the dog as for wilful wounding.

11. "If a man shall smite a house-dog so that it becomes unfit for work, if he shall cut off its ear or its paw, and thereupon a thief or a wolf break in and carry away anything from the house, without the dog giving any warning, the man shall pay for the loss, and he shall pay for the wound of the dog as for wilful wounding."

12. O Maker of the material world, thou Holy One! If a man shall smite a shepherd's dog so that it gives up the ghost and the soul parts from the body, what is the penalty that he shall pay?

Ahura Mazda answered: "Eight hundred stripes with the *Aspahe-astra,* eight hundred stripes with the *Sraosho-karana.*"

13. O Maker of the material world, thou Holy One! If a man shall smite a house-dog so that it gives up the ghost and the soul parts from the body, what is the penalty that he shall pay?

Ahura Mazda answered: "Seven hundred stripes with the *Aspahe-astra,* seven hundred stripes with the *Sraosho-karana.*"

14. O Maker of the material world, thou Holy One! If a man shall smite a *Vohunazga* dog so that it gives up the ghost and the soul parts from the body, what is the penalty that he shall pay?

Ahura Mazda answered: "Six hundred stripes with the *Aspahe-astra,* six hundred stripes with the *Sraosho-karana.*"

15. O Maker of the material world, thou Holy One! If a man shall smite a *Tauruna* dog so that it gives up the ghost and the soul parts from the body, what is the penalty that he shall pay?

Ahura Mazda answered: " Five hundred stripes with the *Aspahe-astra,* five hundred stripes with the *Sraosho-karana."*

16. " This is the penalty for the murder of a *Gazu* dog, of a *Vizu* dog, of a porcupine-dog, of a sharp-toothed weasel, of a swift-running fox; this is the penalty for the murder of any of the creatures of the Good Spirit belonging to the dog kind, except the water-dog."

### III

17. O Maker of the material world, thou Holy One! What is the place of the shepherd's dog?

Ahura Mazda answered: " He comes and goes a *Yugyesti*[6] round about the fold, watching for the thief and the wolf."

18. O Maker of the material world, thou Holy One! What is the place of the house-dog?

Ahura Mazda answered: " He comes and goes a *Hathra* round about the house, watching for the thief and the wolf."

19. O Maker of the material world, thou Holy One! What is the place of the *Vohunazga* dog?

Ahura Mazda answered: " He claims none of those talents, and only seeks for his subsistence." [7]

### IV

20. O Maker of the material world, thou Holy One! If a man give bad food to a shepherd's dog, of what sin does he make himself guilty?

Ahura Mazda answered: " He makes himself guilty of the same guilt as though he should serve bad food to a master of a house of the first rank." [8]

21. O Maker of the material world, thou Holy One! If a man give bad food to a house-dog, of what sin does he make himself guilty?

[6] A distance of sixteen *Hathras* (16,000 paces).

[7] " He can not do the same as the shepherd's dog and the house-dog do, but he catches *Khrafstras* and smites the Nasu."— Commentary. It is " the dog without a master " (*gharib*), the vagrant dog; he is held in great esteem (Section 22), and is one of the dogs which can be used for the Sag-did.

[8] Invited as a guest.

Ahura Mazda answered: " He makes himself guilty of the same guilt as though he should serve bad food to a master of a house of middle rank."

22. O Maker of the material world, thou Holy One! If a man give bad food to a *Vohunazga* dog, of what sin does he make himself guilty?

Ahura Mazda answered: " He makes himself guilty of the same guilt as though he should serve bad food to a holy man, who should come to his house in the character of a priest." [9]

23. O Maker of the material world, thou Holy One! If a man give bad food to a *Tauruna* dog, of what sin does he make himself guilty?

Ahura Mazda answered: " He makes himself guilty of the same guilt as though he should serve bad food to a young man, born of pious parents, and who can already answer for his deeds." [10]

24. O Maker of the material world, thou Holy One! If a man shall give bad food to a shepherd's dog, what is the penalty that he shall pay?

Ahura Mazda answered: " He is a *Peshotanu:* two hundred stripes with the *Aspahe-astra,* two hundred stripes with the *Sraosho-karana."*

25. O Maker of the material world, thou Holy One! If a man shall give bad food to a house-dog, what is the penalty that he shall pay?

Ahura Mazda answered: " Ninety stripes with the *Aspahe-astra,* ninety stripes with the *Sraosho-karana."*

26. O Maker of the material world, thou Holy One! If a man shall give bad food to a *Vohunazga* dog, what is the penalty that he shall pay?

Ahura Mazda answered: " Seventy stripes with the *Aspahe-astra,* seventy stripes with the *Sraosho-karana."*

[9] The *Vohunazga* dog has no domicile, therefore he is not compared with the master of a house, but with a wandering friar, who lives on charity.

[10] Probably, " Who has performed the *nu-zud,* fifteen years old." The young dog enters the community of the faithful at the age of four months, when he is fit for the Sag-did and can expel the Nasu.

27. O Maker of the material world, thou Holy One! If a man shall give bad food to a *Tauruna* dog, what is the penalty that he shall pay?

Ahura Mazda answered: "Fifty stripes with the *Aspahe-astra,* fifty stripes with the *Sraosho-karana.*

28. "For in this material world, O Spitama Zarathushtra! it is the dog, of all the creatures of the Good Spirit, that most quickly decays into age, while not eating near eating people, and watching goods none of which it receives. Bring ye unto him milk and fat with meat; this is the right food for the dog." [11]

### V

29. O Maker of the material world, thou Holy One! If there be in the house of a worshiper of Mazda a mad dog that bites without barking, what shall the worshipers of Mazda do?

30. Ahura Mazda answered: "They shall put a wooden collar around his neck, and they shall tie thereto a muzzle, an *asti* [12] thick if the wood be hard, two *astis* thick if it be soft. To that collar they shall tie it; by the two sides of the collar they shall tie it.

31. "If they shall not do so, and the mad dog bites without barking, smite a sheep or wound a man, the dog shall pay for the wound of the wounded as for wilful murder. [13]

32. "If the dog shall smite a sheep or wound a man, they shall cut off his right ear.

"If he shall smite another sheep or wound another man, they shall cut off his left ear.

33. "If he shall smite a third sheep or wound a third man, they shall make a cut in his right foot. If he shall

---

[11] "Whenever one eats bread one must put aside three mouthfuls and give them to the dog . . . for among all the poor there is none poorer than the dog."— Saddar 31.

[12] A measure of unknown amount. Framji reads *isti*, "a brick" thick.

[13] According to Solon's law, the dog who had bitten a man was to be delivered to him tied up to a block four cubits long. The Book of Deuteronomy orders the ox who has killed a man to be put to death.

smite a fourth sheep or wound a fourth man, they shall make a cut in his left foot.

34. " If he shall for the fifth time smite a sheep or wound a man, they shall cut off his tail.

" Therefore they shall tie a muzzle to the collar; by the two sides of the collar they shall tie it. If they shall not do so, and the mad dog that bites without barking, smite a sheep or wound a man, he shall pay for the wound of the wounded as for wilful murder."

35. O Maker of the material world, thou Holy One! If there be in the house of a worshiper of Mazda a mad dog, who has no scent, what shall the worshipers of Mazda do?

Ahura Mazda answered: " They shall attend him to heal him, in the same manner as they would do for one of the faithful."

36. O Maker of the material world, thou Holy One! If they try to heal him and fail, what shall the worshipers of Mazda do?

37. Ahura Mazda answered: " They shall put a wooden collar around his neck, and they shall tie thereto a muzzle, an *asti* thick if the wood be hard, two *astis* thick if it be soft. To that collar they shall tie it; by the two sides of the collar they shall tie it.

38. " If they shall not do so, the scentless dog may fall into a hole, or a well, or a precipice, or a river, or a canal, and come to grief: if he come to grief so, they shall be therefore *Peshotanus.*

## VI

39. " The dog, O Spitama Zarathushtra! I, Ahura Mazda, have made self-clothed and self-shod; watchful and wakeful; and sharp-toothed; born to take his food from man and to watch over man's goods. I, Ahura Mazda, have made the dog strong of body against the evil-doer, when sound of mind and watchful over your goods.

40. " And whosoever shall awake at his voice, O Spitama Zarathushtra! neither shall the thief nor the wolf carry anything from his house, without his being warned; the wolf

shall be smitten and torn to pieces; he is driven away, he melts away like snow."

## VII

41. O Maker of the material world, thou Holy One! Which of the two wolves deserves more to be killed, the one that a he-dog begets of a she-wolf, or the one that a he-wolf begets of a she-dog?

Ahura Mazda answered: "Of these two wolves, the one that a he-dog begets of a she-wolf deserves more to be killed than the one that a he-wolf begets of a she-dog.

42. "For the dogs born therefrom fall on the shepherd's dog, on the house-dog, on the *Vohunazga* dog, on the trained dog, and destroy the folds; such dogs are more murderous, more mischievous, more destructive to the folds than any other dogs.

43. "And the wolves born therefrom fall on the shepherd's dog, on the house-dog, on the *Vohunazga* dog, on the trained dog, and destroy the folds; such wolves are more murderous, more mischievous, more destructive to the folds than any other wolves.

## VIII

44. "A dog has the character of eight sorts of people:
"He has the character of a priest,
"He has the character of a warrior,
"He has the character of a husbandman,
"He has the character of a strolling singer,
"He has the character of a thief,
"He has the character of a *disu,*
"He has the character of a courtezan,
"He has the character of a child.

45. "He eats the refuse, like a priest; [14] he is easily satisfied,[15] like a priest; he is patient, like a priest; he wants only a small piece of bread, like a priest; in these things he is like unto a priest.

[14] A wandering priest.
[15] "Good treatment makes him joyous."— Commentary.

"He marches in front, like a warrior; he fights for the beneficent cow, like a warrior; [16] he goes first out of the house, like a warrior; [17] in these things he is like unto a warrior.

46. "He is watchful and sleeps lightly, like a husbandman; he goes first out of the house, like a husbandman; [18] he returns last into the house, like a husbandman; [19] in these things he is like unto a husbandman.

"He is fond of singing, like a strolling singer; [20] he wounds him who gets too near, [21] like a strolling singer; he is ill-trained, like a strolling singer; he is changeful, like a strolling singer; in these things he is like unto a strolling singer.

47. "He is fond of darkness, like a thief; he prowls about in darkness, like a thief; he is a shameless eater, like a thief; he is therefore an unfaithful keeper, like a thief; [22] in these things he is like unto a thief.

"He is fond of darkness, like a *disu;* [23] he prowls about in darkness, like a *disu;* he is a shameless eater, like a *disu;* he is therefore an unfaithful keeper, like a *disu;* in these things he is like unto a *disu.*

48. "He is fond of singing, like a courtezan; he wounds him who gets too near, like a courtezan; he roams along the roads, like a courtezan; he is ill-trained, like a courtezan; he is changeful, like a courtezan; [24] in these things he is like unto a courtezan.

"He is fond of sleep, like a child; he is tender like snow,

---

[16] "He keeps away the wolf and the thief."— Commentary.

[17] This clause is, as it seems, repeated here by mistake from Section 46.

[18] When taking the cattle out of the stables.

[19] When bringing the cattle back to the stables.

[20] The so-called *Looris* of nowadays.

[21] He insults or robs the passer-by, like a *Loori.*—"The *Looris* wander in the world, seeking their life, bed-fellows and fellow-travelers of the dogs and the wolves, ever on the roads to rob day and night."— Firdausi.

[22] "When one trusts him with something, he eats it up."— Commentary.

[23] According to Framji, "a wild beast."

[24] The description of the courtezan follows closely that of the singer: in the East a public songstress is generally a prostitute. *Loori* means both a singer and a prostitute.

like a child; he is full of tongue, like a child; he digs the earth with his paws, like a child; in these things he is like unto a child.

## IX

49. "If those two dogs of mine, the shepherd's dog and the house-dog, pass by any of my houses, let them never be kept away from it.

"For no house could subsist on the earth made by Ahura, but for those two dogs of mine, the shepherd's dog and the house-dog." [25]

## X

50. O Maker of the material world, thou Holy One! When a dog dies, with marrow and seed dried up, whereto does his ghost go?

51. Ahura Mazda answered: "It passes to the spring of the waters, O Spitama Zarathushtra! and there out of them two water-dogs are formed: out of every thousand dogs and every thousand she-dogs, a couple is formed, a water-dog and a water she-dog.

52. "He who kills a water-dog brings about a drought that dries up pastures.

"Until then, O Spitama Zarathushtra! sweetness and fatness would flow out from that land and from those fields, with health and healing, with fulness and increase and growth, and a growing of corn and grass."

53. O Maker of the material world, thou Holy One! When are sweetness and fatness to come back again to that land and to those fields, with health and healing, with fulness and increase and growth, and a growing of corn and grass?

54, 55. Ahura Mazda answered: "Sweetness and fatness will never come back again to that land and to those fields, with health and healing, with fulness and increase and growth, and a growing of corn and grass, until the murderer of the water-dog has been smitten to death on the spot, and the holy soul of the dog has been offered up a sacrifice, for

[25] "But for the dog not a single head of cattle would remain in existence."— Saddar 31.

three days and three nights, with fire blazing, with *Baresma* tied up, and with *Haoma* prepared.

56. " Then sweetness and fatness will come back again to that land and to those fields, with health and healing, with fulness and increase and growth, and a growing of corn and grass."

FARGARD XIV.— (THE DOG)[1]

1. Zarathushtra asked Ahura Mazda: " O Ahura Mazda, most beneficent Spirit, Maker of the material world, thou Holy One! He who smites one of those water-dogs that are born one from a thousand dogs and a thousand she-dogs,[2] so that he gives up the ghost and the soul parts from the body, what is the penalty that he shall pay ? "

2. Ahura Mazda answered: " He shall pay ten thousand stripes with the *Aspahe-astra,* ten thousand stripes with the *Sraosho-karana.*[3]

" He shall godly and piously bring unto the fire of Ahura Mazda[4] ten thousand loads of hard, well dried, well examined[5] wood, to redeem his own soul.

3. " He shall godly and piously bring unto the fire of

---

[1] This Fargard is nothing more than an appendix to the last clause in the preceding Fargard (Section 50 *seq.*). How the murder of a water-dog (an otter) may be atoned for is described in it at full length. The extravagance of the penalties prescribed may well make it doubtful whether the legislation of the Vendidad had ever any substantial existence in practise. These exorbitant prescriptions seem to be intended only to impress on the mind of the faithful the heinousness of the offense to be avoided.

[2] See preceding Fargard, Section 51.

[3] He shall pay 50 *tanafuhrs* ( = 15,000 *istirs* = 60,000 *dirhems*). " If he can afford it, he will atone in the manner stated in the Avesta; if he can not afford it, it will be sufficient to perform a complete *Izasne* (sacrifice)."— Commentary.

[4] To the altar of the Bahram fire.

[5] " It is forbidden to take any ill-smelling thing to the fire and to kindle it thereon; it is forbidden to kindle green wood, and even though the wood were hard and dry, one must examine it three times, lest there may be any hair or any unclean matter upon it."— Gr. Rav. Although the pious Arda Viraf had always taken the utmost care never to put on the fire any wood but such as was seven years old, yet, when he entered Paradise, Atar, the genius of fire, showed him reproachfully a large tank full of the water which that wood had exuded (see Arda Viraf x).

Ahura Mazda ten thousand loads of soft wood, of *Urvasna, Vohu-gaona, Vohu-kereti, Hadha-naepata,* or any sweet-scented plant, to redeem his own soul.

4. "He shall godly and piously tie ten thousand bundles of *Baresma,* to redeem his own soul.

"He shall offer up to the Good Waters ten thousand *Zaothra* libations with the *Haoma* and the milk, cleanly prepared and well strained, cleanly prepared and well strained by a pious man, and mixed with the roots of the tree known as *Hadha-naepata,* to redeem his own soul.

5. "He shall kill ten thousand snakes of those that go upon the belly. He shall kill ten thousand Kahrpus, who are snakes with the shape of a dog. He shall kill ten thousand tortoises. He shall kill ten thousand land-frogs; he shall kill ten thousand water-frogs. He shall kill ten thousand corn-carrying ants; he shall kill ten thousand ants of the small, venomous, mischievous kind.

6. "He shall kill ten thousand worms of those that live on dirt; he shall kill ten thousand raging flies.

"He shall fill up ten thousand holes for the unclean.

"He shall godly and piously give to godly men twice the set of seven implements for the fire, to redeem his own soul, namely:

7. "The two answering implements for fire; a broom; a pair of tongs; a pair of round bellows extended at the bottom, contracted at the top; a sharp-edged sharp-pointed adze; a sharp-toothed sharp-pointed saw; by means of which the worshipers of Mazda procure wood for the fire of Ahura Mazda.

8. "He shall godly and piously give to godly men a set of the priestly instruments of which the priests make use, to redeem his own soul, namely: The *Astra;* the meat vessel; the *Paitidana;*[6] the *Khrafstraghna;*[7] the *Sraosho-karana;*

[6] As everything that goes out of man is unclean, his breath defiles all that it touches; priests, therefore, while on duty, and even laymen, while praying or eating, must wear a mouth-veil, the *Paitidana,* consisting "of two pieces of white cotton cloth, hanging loosely from the bridge of the nose to, at least, two inches below the mouth, and tied with two strings at the back of the head."

[7] The "*Khrafstra*-killer"; an instrument for killing snakes, etc. It

the cup for the *Myazda;* the cups for mixing and dividing; the regular mortar; the *Haoma* cups; and the *Baresma.*

9. " He shall godly and piously give to godly men a set of all the war-implements of which the warriors make use, to redeem his own soul;

" The first being a javelin, the second a sword, the third a club, the fourth a bow, the fifth a saddle with a quiver and thirty brass-headed arrows, the sixth a sling with arm-string and with thirty sling stones;

" The seventh a cuirass, the eighth a hauberk, the ninth a tunic, the tenth a helmet, the eleventh a girdle, the twelfth a pair of greaves.

10. " He shall godly and piously give to godly men a set of all the implements of which the husbandmen make use, to redeem his own soul, namely:  A plow with yoke and . . .; a goad for ox; a mortar of stone; a round-headed hand-mill for grinding corn;

11. " A spade for digging and tilling; one measure of silver and one measure of gold."

O Maker of the material world, thou Holy One!  How much silver?

Ahura Mazda answered: " The price of a stallion."

O Maker of the material world, thou Holy One!  How much gold?

Ahura Mazda answered: " The price of a he-camel.

12. " He shall godly and piously procure a rill of running water [8] for godly husbandmen, to redeem his own soul."

O Maker of the material world, thou Holy One!  How large is the rill?

Ahura Mazda answered: " The depth of a dog, and the breadth of a dog.[9]

13. " He shall godly and piously give a piece of arable land to godly men, to redeem his own soul."

is a stick with a leather thong at its end, something like the Indian fly-flap.

[8] The most precious of all gifts in such a dry place as Iran.  Water is obtained either through canals of derivation or through underground canals (*karez, kanat*).

[9] Which is estimated " a foot deep, a foot broad."— Commentary.

O Maker of the material world, thou Holy One! How large is the piece of land?

Ahura Mazda answered: "As much as can be watered with such a rill divided into two canals.

14. "He shall godly and piously procure for godly men a stable for oxen, with nine *hathras* and nine *nematas,*[10] to redeem his own soul."

O Maker of the material world, thou Holy One! How large is the stable?

Ahura Mazda answered: "It shall have twelve alleys [11] in the largest part of the house, nine alleys in the middle part, six alleys in the smallest part.

"He shall godly and piously give to godly men goodly beds with sheets and cushions, to redeem his own soul.

15. "He shall godly and piously give in marriage to a godly man a virgin maid, whom no man has known,[12] to redeem his own soul."

O Maker of the material world, thou Holy One! What sort of maid?

Ahura Mazda answered: "A sister or a daughter of his, at the age of puberty, with earrings in her ears, and past her fifteenth year.

16. "He shall godly and piously give to holy men twice seven head of small cattle, to redeem his own soul.

"He shall bring up twice seven whelps.

"He shall throw twice seven bridges over canals.

17. "He shall put into repair twice nine stables that are out of repair.

"He shall cleanse twice nine dogs from *stipti, anairiti,* and *vyangura,*[13] and all the diseases that are produced on the body of a dog.

"He shall treat twice nine godly men to their fill of meat, bread, strong drink, and wine.

18. "This is the penalty, this is the atonement which

10 Meaning unknown.
11 Twelve ranks of stalls (?).
12 Match-making is a good work.— Fargard IV, 44.
13 Meaning unknown.

saves the faithful man who submits to it, not him who does not submit to it. Such a one shall surely be an inhabitant in the mansion of the Druj.

## FARGARD XV.— (ON SIN)

### I

1. How many are the sins that men commit and that, being committed and not confessed, nor atoned for, make their committer a *Peshotanu?* [1]

2. Ahura Mazda answered: "There are five such sins, O holy Zarathushtra! It is the first of these sins that men commit when a man teaches one of the faithful another faith, another law,[2] a lower doctrine, and he leads him astray with a full knowledge and conscience of the sin: the man who has done the deed becomes a *Peshotanu.*

3. "It is the second of these sins when a man gives bones too hard or food too hot to a shepherd's dog or to a house-dog;

4. "If the bones stick in the dog's teeth or stop in his throat; or if the food too hot burn his mouth or his tongue, he may come to grief thereby; if he come to grief thereby, the man who has done the deed becomes a *Peshotanu.*[3]

5. "It is the third of these sins when a man smites a bitch big with young or affrights her by running after her, or shouting or clapping with the hands;

6. "If the bitch fall into a hole, or a well, or a precipice, or a river, or a canal, she may come to grief thereby; if she come to grief thereby, the man who has done the deed becomes a *Peshotanu.*

7. "It is the fourth of these sins when a man has intercourse with a woman who has the whites or sees the blood, the man that has done the deed becomes a *Peshotanu.*

8. "It is the fifth of these sins when a man has intercourse

---

[1] That is to say: he shall receive two hundred strokes with the *Aspahe-astra* or the *Sraosho-karana;* or pay three hundred *istirs.*

[2] The Commentary has, "that is, a creed that is not ours."

[3] He who gives too hot food to a dog so as to burn his throat is *margarzan* (guilty of death); he who gives bones to a dog so as to tear his throat is *margarzan.*— Gr. Rav. 639.

with a woman quick with child, whether the milk has already
come to her breasts or has not yet come: she may come to
grief thereby; if she come to grief thereby, the man who has
done the deed becomes a *Peshotanu*.

## II a

9. " If a man come near unto a damsel, either dependent
on the chief of the family or not dependent, either delivered
unto a husband or not delivered, and she conceives by him,
let her not, being ashamed of the people, produce in herself
the menses, against the course of nature, by means of water
and plants.

10. "And if the damsel, being ashamed of the people,
shall produce in herself the menses against the course of
nature, by means of water and plants, it is a fresh sin as
heavy as the first.

11. " If a man come near unto a damsel, either dependent
on the chief of the family or not dependent, either delivered
unto a husband or not delivered, and she conceives by him,
let her not, being ashamed of the people, destroy the fruit in
her womb.

12. " And if the damsel, being ashamed of the people, shall
destroy the fruit in her womb, the sin is on both the father
and herself, the murder is on both the father and herself;
both the father and herself shall pay the penalty for wilful
murder.

## II b

13. " If a man come near unto a damsel, either dependent
on the chief of the family or not dependent, either delivered
unto a husband or not delivered, and she conceives by him,
and she says, ' I have conceived by thee '; and he replies,
' Go then to the old woman [4] and apply to her for one of
her drugs, that she may procure thee miscarriage ';

14. " And the damsel goes to the old woman and applies
to her for one of her drugs, that she may procure her a miscarriage; and the old woman brings her some *Banga*, or

[4] The nurse (Framji), or the midwife.

*Shaeta,* a drug that kills in the womb or one that expels out
of the womb, or some other of the drugs that produce miscarriage, and the man says, ' Cause thy fruit to perish!'
and she causes her fruit to perish; the sin is on the head of
all three, the man, the damsel, and the old woman.

15. " If a man come near unto a damsel, either dependent
on the chief of the family or not dependent, either delivered
unto a husband or not delivered, and she conceives by him,
so long shall he support her, until the child be born.

16. " If he shall not support her, so that the child comes
to grief, for want of proper support, he shall pay for it the
penalty for wilful murder."

17. O Maker of the material world, thou Holy One! If
she be near her time, which is the worshiper of Mazda that
shall support her?

18. Ahura Mazda answered: " If a man come near unto a
damsel, either dependent on the chief of the family or not
dependent, either delivered unto a husband or not delivered,
and she conceives by him, so long shall he support her, until
the child be born.

19. " If he shall not support her . . ."[5]

" It lies with the faithful to look in the same way after
every pregnant female, either two-footed or four-footed, two-
footed woman or four-footed bitch."

### III

20. O Maker of the material world, thou Holy One! If a
bitch be near her time, which is the worshiper of Mazda
that shall support her?

21. Ahura Mazda answered: " He whose house stands
nearest, the care of supporting her is his; so long shall he
support her, until the whelps be born.

22. " If he shall not support her, so that the whelps come
to grief, for want of proper support, he shall pay for it the
penalty for wilful murder."

23. O Maker of the material world, thou Holy One! If

[5] The sentence is left unfinished: Framji fills it with the words in
Section 16, " so that the child," etc.

a bitch be near her time and be lying in a stable for camels, which is the worshiper of Mazda that shall support her?

24. Ahura Mazda answered: "He who built the stable for camels or whoso holds it,[6] the care of supporting her is his; so long shall he support her, until the whelps be born.

25. "If he shall not support her, so that the whelps come to grief, for want of proper support, he shall pay for it the penalty for wilful murder."

26. O Maker of the material world, thou Holy One! If a bitch be near her time and be lying in a stable for horses, which is the worshiper of Mazda that shall support her?

27. Ahura Mazda answered: "He who built the stable for horses or whoso holds it, the care of supporting her is his; so long shall he support her, until the whelps be born.

28. "If he shall not support her, so that the whelps come to grief, for want of proper support, he shall pay for it the penalty for wilful murder."

29. O Maker of the material world, thou Holy One! If a bitch be near her time and be lying in a stable for oxen, which is the worshiper of Mazda that shall support her?

30. Ahura Mazda answered: "He who built the stable for oxen or whoso holds it, the care of supporting her is his; so long shall he support her, until the whelps be born.

31. "If he shall not support her, so that the whelps come to grief, for want of proper support, he shall pay for it the penalty for wilful murder."

32. O Maker of the material world, thou Holy One! If a bitch be near her time and be lying in a sheep-fold, which is the worshiper of Mazda that shall support her?

33. Ahura Mazda answered: "He who built the sheep-fold or whoso holds it, the care of supporting her is his; so long shall he support her, until the whelps be born.

34. "If he shall not support her so that the whelps come to grief, for want of proper support, he shall pay for it the penalty for wilful murder."

35. O Maker of the material world, thou Holy One! If a bitch be near her time and be lying on the earth-wall,[7]

[6] "In pledge or for rent."— Framji.    [7] The wall around the house.

which is the worshiper of Mazda that shall support her?

36. Ahura Mazda answered: "He who erected the wall or whoso holds it, the care of supporting her is his; so long shall he support her, until the whelps be born.

37. "If he shall not support her, so that the whelps come to grief, for want of proper support, he shall pay for it the penalty for wilful murder."

38. O Maker of the material world, thou Holy One! If a bitch be near her time and be lying in the moat,[8] which is the worshiper of Mazda that shall support her?

39. Ahura Mazda answered: "He who dug the moat or whoso holds it, the care of supporting her is his; so long shall he support her, until the whelps be born.

40. "If he shall not support her, so that the whelps come to grief, for want of proper support, he shall pay for it the penalty for wilful murder."

41. O Maker of the material world, thou Holy One! If a bitch be near her time and be lying in the middle of a pasture-field, which is the worshiper of Mazda that shall support her?

42. Ahura Mazda answered: "He who sowed the pasture-field or whoso holds it, the care of supporting her is his; so long shall he support her, until the whelps be born. If he shall not support her, so that the whelps come to grief, for want of proper support, he shall pay for it the penalty for wilful murder.

43. "He shall take her to rest upon a litter of *nemovanta* or of any foliage fit for a litter; so long shall he support her, until the young dogs are capable of self-defense and self-subsistence."

44. O Maker of the material world, thou Holy One! When are the dogs capable of self-defense and self-subsistence?

45. Ahura Mazda answered: "When they are able to run about in a circuit of twice seven houses around. Then they may be let loose, whether it be winter or summer.

[8] The moat before the earth-wall.

"Young dogs ought to be supported for six months, children for seven years.

"Atar,[9] the son of Ahura Mazda, watches as well over a pregnant bitch as he does over a woman."

## IV

46. O Maker of the material world, thou Holy One! If worshipers of Mazda want to have a bitch so covered that the offspring shall be one of a strong nature, what shall they do?

47. Ahura Mazda answered: "They shall dig a hole in the earth, in the middle of the fold, half a foot deep if the earth be hard, half the height of a man if the earth be soft.

48. "They shall first tie up the bitch there, far from children and from the Fire, the son of Ahura Mazda,[10] and they shall watch by her until a dog comes there from anywhere; then another again, and then a third again, each being kept apart from the former, lest they should assail one another.

49. "The bitch being thus covered by three dogs, grows big with young and the milk comes to her teats and she brings forth a young one that is born from several dogs."

50. If a man smite a bitch who has been covered by three dogs, and who has already milk, and who shall bring forth a young one born from several dogs, what is the penalty that he shall pay?

51. Ahura Mazda answered: "Seven hundred stripes with the *Aspahe-astra*, seven hundred stripes with the *Sraosho-karana*."

[9] "When a woman becomes pregnant in a house, it is necessary to make an endeavor so that there may be a continual fire in that house, and to maintain a good watch over it. And, when the child becomes separate from the mother, it is necessary to burn a lamp for three nights and days — if they burn a fire it would be better — so that the demons and fiends may not be able to do any damage and harm; because, when a child is born, it is exceedingly delicate for those three days."— Saddar xvi; West, Pahlavi Texts, iii, 277.

[10] "From children, lest she shall bite them; from the fire, lest it shall hurt her."— Commentary.

## FARGARD XVI.—(ON WOMEN)

### I

1. O Maker of the material world, thou Holy One!  If there be in the house of a worshiper of Mazda a woman who has the whites or sees blood, what shall the worshipers of Mazda do?

2. Ahura Mazda answered: " They shall clear the way of the wood there, both plants and trees; they shall strew dry dust on the ground; and they shall isolate a half, or a third, or a fourth, or a fifth part of the house,[1] lest her look should fall upon the fire."

3. O Maker of the material world, thou Holy One!  How far from the fire?  How far from the water?  How far from the consecrated bundles of *Baresma?*  How far from the faithful?

4. Ahura Mazda answered: " Fifteen paces from the fire, fifteen paces from the water, fifteen paces from the consecrated bundles of *Baresma,* three paces from the faithful."

5. O Maker of the material world, thou Holy One!  How far from her shall he stay, who brings food to a woman who has the whites or sees the blood?

6. Ahura Mazda answered: " Three paces[2] from her shall he stay, who brings food to a woman who has the whites or sees the blood."

In what kind of vessels shall he bring her bread?  In what kind of vessels shall he bring her barley-drink?

" In vessels of brass, or of lead, or of any common metal."[3]

7. How much bread shall he bring to her?  How much barley-drink shall he bring?

" Two *danares*[4] of dry bread, and one *danare* of liquor, lest she should get too weak.

---

[1] Nowadays a room on the ground-floor is reserved for that use.

[2] The food is held out to her from a distance in a metal spoon.

[3] Earthen vessels, when defiled, can not be made clean; but metal vessels can.

[4] A *danare* is, according to Anquetil, as much as four *tolas;* a *tola* is from 105 to 175 grains.

" If a child has just touched her, they shall first wash his hands and then his body.

## II

8. " If she still see blood after three nights have passed, she shall sit in the place of infirmity until four nights have passed.

" If she still see blood after four nights have passed, she shall sit in the place of infirmity until five nights have passed.

" If she still see blood after five nights have passed, she shall sit in the place of infirmity until six nights have passed.

" If she still see blood after six nights have passed, she shall sit in the place of infirmity until seven nights have passed.

10. " If she still see blood after seven nights have passed, she shall sit in the place of infirmity until eight nights have passed.

" If she still see blood after eight nights have passed, she shall sit in the place of infirmity until nine nights have passed.

11. " If she still see blood after nine nights have passed, this is a work of the Daevas which they have performed for the worship and glorification of the Daevas.

" The worshipers of Mazda shall clear the way of the wood there, both plants and trees;

12. " They shall dig three holes in the earth, and they shall wash the woman with *gomez* by two of those holes and with water by the third.

" They shall kill *Khrafstras*, to wit: two hundred corn-carrying ants, if it be summer; two hundred of any other sort of the *Khrafstras* made by Angra Mainyu, if it be winter."

## III

13. If a worshiper of Mazda shall suppress the issue of a woman who has the whites or sees blood, what is the penalty that he shall pay?

Ahura Mazda answered: " He is a *Peshotanu:* two hundred stripes with the *Aspahe-astra,* two hundred stripes with the *Sraosho-karana."*

14. O Maker of the material world, thou Holy One! If a man shall again and again lasciviously touch the body of a woman who has the whites or sees blood, so that the whites turn to the blood or the blood turns to the whites, what is the penalty that he shall pay?

15. Ahura Mazda answered: " For the first time he comes near unto her, for the first time he lies by her, thirty stripes with the *Aspahe-astra,* thirty stripes with the *Sraosho-karana.*

" For the second time he comes near unto her, for the second time he lies by her, fifty stripes with the *Aspahe-astra,* fifty stripes with the *Sraosho-karana.*

" For the third time he comes near unto her, for the third time he lies by her, seventy stripes with the *Aspahe-astra,* seventy stripes with the *Sraosho-karana."*

16. For the fourth time he comes near unto her, for the fourth time he lies by her, if he shall press the body under her clothes, if he shall go in between the unclean thighs, but without sexual intercourse, what is the penalty that he shall pay?

Ahura Mazda answered: " Ninety stripes with the *Aspahe-astra,* ninety stripes with the *Sraosho-karana.*

17. " Whosoever shall lie in sexual intercouse with a woman who has the whites or sees blood, does no better deed than if he should burn the corpse of his own son, born of his own body and dead of *naeza,* and drop its fat into the fire.

18. " All wicked, embodiments of the Druj, are scorners of the judge: all scorners of the judge are rebels against the Sovereign: all rebels against the Sovereign are ungodly men; and all ungodly men are worthy of death."

## FARGARD XVII.— (HAIR AND NAILS)[1]

### I

1. Zarathushtra asked Ahura Mazda: "O Ahura Mazda, most beneficent Spirit, Maker of the material world, thou Holy One! Which is the most deadly deed whereby a man offers up a sacrifice to the Daevas?"[2]

2. Ahura Mazda answered: "It is when a man here below, combing his hair or shaving it off, or paring off his nails, drops them[3] in a hole or in a crack.

3. "Then by this transgression of the rites, Daevas are produced in the earth; by this transgression of the rites, those *Khrafstras* are produced in the earth which men call lice, and which eat up the corn in the corn-field and the clothes in the wardrobe.

4. "Therefore, thou, O Zarathushtra! whenever here below thou shalt comb thy hair or shave it off, or pare off thy nails, thou shalt take them away ten paces from the faithful, twenty paces from the fire, thirty paces from the water, fifty paces from the consecrated bundles of *Baresma*.

5. "Then thou shalt dig a hole, a *disti* deep if the earth be hard, a *vitasti* deep if it be soft; thou shalt take the hair down there and thou shalt say aloud these victorious words: 'For him, as a reward, Mazda made the plants grow up.'

6. "Thereupon thou shalt draw three furrows with a knife of metal around the hole, or six furrows or nine, and thou shalt chant the Ahuna-Vairya three times, or six, or nine.

### II

7. "For the nails, thou shalt dig a hole, out of the house, as deep as the top joint of the little finger; thou shalt take

---

[1] Anything that has been separated from the body of man is considered dead matter (*nasu*), and is accordingly unclean. As soon as hair and nails are cut off, the demon takes hold of them and has to be driven away from them by spells, in the same way as he is from the bodies of the dead.

[2] Any offense to religion is considered an offering to the Daevas, whose strength is thereby increased.

[3] Without performing the requisite ceremonies.

the nails down there and thou shalt say aloud these victorious words: 'The things that the pure proclaim through Asha and Vohu-mano.'

8. "Then thou shalt draw three furrows with a knife of metal around the hole, or six furrows or nine, and thou shalt chant the Ahuna-Vairya three times, or six, or nine.

9. "And then: 'O Asho-zusta bird![4] these nails I announce and consecrate unto thee. May they be for thee so many spears and knives, so many bows and falcon-winged arrows, and so many sling-stones against the Mazainya Daevas!'

10. "If those nails have not been consecrated to the bird, they shall be in the hands of the Mazainya Daevas so many spears and knives, so many bows and falcon-winged arrows, and so many sling-stones against the Mazainya Daevas.

11. "All wicked embodiments of the Druj are scorners of the judge: all scorners of the judge are rebels against the Sovereign: all rebels against the Sovereign are ungodly men; and all ungodly men are worthy of death."

### FARGARD XVIII.— (ON SINS)

## I

1. "There is many a one, O holy Zarathushtra!" said Ahura Mazda, "who wears a wrong *Paitidana*,[1] and who has not girded his loins with the Religion; when such a man says, 'I am an Athravan,' he lies; do not call him an Athravan, O holy Zarathushtra!" thus said Ahura Mazda.

2. "He holds a wrong *Khrafstraghna*[2] in his hand and he has not girded his loins with the Religion; when he says, 'I am an Athravan,' he lies; do not call him an Athravan, O holy Zarathushtra!" thus said Ahura Mazda.

3. "He holds a wrong twig in his hand and he has not girded his loins with the Religion; when he says, 'I am an

[4] "The owl," according to modern tradition. The word literally means "friend of holiness."

[1] Face-veil.

[2] Snake-killer.

Athravan,' he lies; do not call him an Athravan, O holy Zarathushtra!" thus said Ahura Mazda.

4. "He wields a wrong *Astra mairya*[3] and he has not girded his loins with the Religion; when he says, 'I am an Athravan,' he lies; do not call him an Athravan, O holy Zarathushtra!" thus said Ahura Mazda.

5. "He who sleeps on throughout the night, neither performing the Yasna nor chanting the hymns, worshiping neither by word nor by deed, neither learning nor teaching, with a longing for everlasting life, he lies when he says, 'I am an Athravan,' do not call him an Athravan, O holy Zarathushtra!' thus said Ahura Mazda.

6. "Him thou shalt call an Athravan, O holy Zarathushtra! who throughout the night sits up and demands of the holy Wisdom,[4] which makes man free from anxiety, and wide of heart, and easy of conscience at the head of the Kinvat bridge,[5] and which makes him reach that world, that holy world, that excellent world of Paradise.

7. "Therefore demand of me, thou upright one! of me, who am the Maker, the most beneficent of all beings, the best knowing, the most pleased in answering what is asked of me; demand of me, that thou mayst be the better, that thou mayst be the happier."

8. Zarathushtra asked Ahura Mazda: "O Maker of the material world, thou Holy One! What is it that brings in the unseen power of Death?"

9. Ahura Mazda answered: "It is the man that teaches a wrong Religion; it is the man who continues for three springs without wearing the sacred girdle,[6] without chanting the Gathas, without worshiping the Good Waters.

[3] The *astra* (*Aspahe-astra*) with which the priest, as a *Sraosha-varez*, chastises the guilty.

[4] That is to say, studies the law and learns from those who know it.

[5] See Fargard xix, 30. "It gives him a stout heart, when standing before the Kinvat bridge."— Commentary.

[6] The *Kosti*, which must be worn by every Parsi, man or woman, from their fifteenth year of age (see below, Section 54 *seq.*); it is the badge of the faithful, the girdle by which he is united both with Ormazd and with his fellow-believers.

10. "And he who should set that man at liberty, when bound in prison, does no better deed than if he should cut a man's head off his neck.

11. "For the blessing uttered by a wicked, ungodly *Ashe-maogha* does not go past the mouth of the blesser; the blessing of two *Ashemaoghas* does not go past the tongue; the blessing of three is nothing; the blessing of four [7] turns to self-cursing.

12. "Whosoever should give to a wicked, ungodly *Ashe-maogha* either some *Haoma* prepared, or some *Myazda* consecrated with blessings, does no better deed than if he should lead a thousand horse against the boroughs of the worshipers of Mazda, and should slaughter the men thereof, and drive off the cattle as plunder.

13. "Demand of me, thou upright one! of me, who am the Maker, the most beneficent of all beings, the best knowing, the most pleased in answering what is asked of me; demand of me, that thou mayst be the better, that thou mayst be the happier."

## II

14. Zarathushtra asked Ahura Mazda: "Who is the Sraosha-varez [8] of Sraosha? the holy, strong Sraosha, who is Obedience incarnate, a Sovereign with an astounding weapon." [9]

15. Ahura Mazda answered: "It is the bird named *Parodars*,[10] which ill-speaking people call *Kahrkatas*,[11] O

[7] Perhaps better: "The second . . ., the third . . ., the fourth blessing of an *Ashemaogha*."

[8] "Who is he who sets the world in motion?"— Commentary.

[9] Sraosha, *Srosh*, the Genius of Active Piety. He first tied the *Baresma*, sacrificed to Ahura, and sang the Gathas. Thrice in each day and each night he descends upon the earth to smite Angra Mainyu and his crew of demons. With his club uplifted he protects the world from the demons of the night, and the dead from the terrors of death and from the assaults of Angra Mainyu and Asto-vidotu. It is through a sacrifice performed by Ormazd, as a Zoti, and Srosh, as a Raspi, that at the end of time Ahriman will be forever vanquished and brought to naught.

[10] "He who foreshows the coming dawn; the cock."

[11] "When he is not called so, he is powerful."— Commentary.

holy Zarathushtra! the bird that lifts up his voice against the mighty *Ushah:* [12]

16. "'Arise, O men! recite the *Ashem yad vahistem* that smites down the Daevas.[13] Lo! here is Bushyasta, the long-handed,[14] coming upon you, who lulls to sleep again the whole living world, as soon as it has awaked: "Sleep!" she says, "O poor man! the time [15] is not yet come."

17. "'On the three excellent things be never intent, namely, good thoughts, good words, and good deeds; on the three abominable things be ever intent, namely, bad thoughts, bad words, and bad deeds.'

18. "On the first part of the night, Atar, the son of Ahura Mazda, calls the master of the house for help, saying:

19. "'Up! arise, thou master of the house! put on thy girdle on thy clothes, wash thy hands, take wood, bring it unto me, and let me burn bright with the clean wood, carried by thy well-washed hands.[16] Here comes Azi,[17] made by the Daevas, who consumes me and wants to put me out of the world.'

20. "On the second part of the night, Atar, the son of Ahura Mazda, calls the husbandman for help, saying:

21. "'Up! arise, thou husbandman! Put on thy girdle on thy clothes, wash thy hands, take wood, bring it unto me, and let me burn bright with the clean wood, carried by thy

[12] *Ushah,* the second half of the night, from midnight to the dawn.

[13] The cock is "the drum of the world." As crowing in the dawn that dazzles away the fiends, he crows away the demons: "The cock was created to fight against the fiends and wizards; ... he is with the dog an ally of Srosh against demons."—Bundahis xix. "No demon can enter a house in which there is a cock; and, above all, should this bird come to the residence of a demon, and move his tongue to chant the praises of the glorious and exalted Creator, that instant the evil spirit takes to flight."—Mirkhond.

[14] The demon of sleep, laziness, procrastination. She lulls back to sleep the world as soon as awaked, and makes the faithful forget in slumber the hour of prayer.

[15] "To perform thy religious duties."—Commentary.

[16] The Parsi, as soon as he has risen, must put on the *Kosti,* wash his hands, and put wood on the fire.

[17] Azi, the demon of avidity; he extinguishes the fire, while he devours the wood.

well-washed hands.   Here comes Azi, made by the Daevas, who consumes me and wants to put me out of the world.'

22. "On the third part of the night, Atar, the son of Ahura Mazda, calls the holy Sraosha for help, saying: 'Come thou, holy, well-formed Sraosha, (then he brings unto me some clean wood with his well-washed hands.)[18]  Here comes Azi, made by the Daevas, who consumes me and wants to put me out of the world.'

23. "And then the holy Sraosha wakes up the bird named *Parodars,* which ill-speaking people call *Kahrkatas,* and the bird lifts up his voice against the mighty *Ushah:*

24. "'Arise, O men! recite the *Ashem yad vahistem* and the *Naismi daevo.*[19]   Lo! here is Bushyasta, the long-handed, coming upon you, who lulls to sleep again the whole living world as soon as it has awaked: "Sleep!" she says, "O poor man! the time is not yet come."

25. "'On the three excellent things be never intent, namely, good thoughts, good words, and good deeds; on the three abominable things be ever intent, namely, bad thoughts, bad words, and bad deeds.'

26. "And then bed-fellows address one another:  'Rise up, here is the cock calling me up.'  Which ever of the two first gets up shall first enter Paradise: whichever of the two shall first, with well-washed hands, bring clean wood unto Atar, the son of Ahura Mazda, Atar, well pleased with him and not angry, and fed as is required, will thus bless him:

27. "'May herds of oxen and sons accrue to thee: may thy mind be master of its vow, may thy soul be master of its vow, and mayst thou live on in the joy of thy soul all the nights of thy life.'

"This is the blessing which Atar speaks unto him who brings him dry wood, well examined by the light of the day, well cleansed with godly intent.

28. "And whosoever will kindly and piously present one

---

[18] The text seems to be corrupt: it must probably be emended into "bring into me . . ."

[19] The prayer: "Righteousness is the best of all good . . ." (the *Ashem vohu*), and the profession of faith: "I scorn the Daevas . . ."

of the faithful with a pair of these my *Parodars* birds, a
male and a female, O Spitama Zarathushtra! it is as though
he had given [20] a house with a hundred columns, a thousand
beams, ten thousand large windows, ten thousand small
windows.

29. "And whosoever shall give meat to one of the faithful,
as much of it as the body of this *Parodars* bird of mine, I,
Ahura Mazda, need not interrogate him twice; he shall
directly go to Paradise."

### III

30. The holy Sraosha, letting his club down upon her,
asked the Druj: "O thou wretched, worthless Druj! Thou
then, alone in the material world, dost bear offspring without
any male coming unto thee?"

31. The Druj demon answered: "O holy, well-formed
Sraosha! It is not so, nor do I, alone in the material world,
bear offspring without any male coming unto me.

32. "For there are four males of mine; and they make
me conceive progeny as other males make their females
conceive by their seed." [21]

33. The holy Sraosha, letting his club down upon her,
asked the Druj: "O thou wretched, worthless Druj! Who
is the first of those males of thine?"

34. The Druj demon answered: "O holy, well-formed
Sraosha! He is the first of my males who, being entreated
by one of the faithful, does not give him anything, be it ever
so little, of the riches he has treasured up. [22]

35. "That man makes me conceive progeny as other males
make their females conceive by their seed."

36. The holy Sraosha, letting his club down upon her,
asked the Druj: "O thou wretched, worthless Druj! What
is the thing that can undo that?"

[20] "In the day of recompense."— Commentary. He shall be rewarded
as though he had given a house, etc. . . . he shall receive such a house
in Paradise.

[21] Sin makes the Druj mother of a spontaneous progeny, as the sinner
is "the brood of the Druj."

[22] Compare Fargard III, 34.

37. The Druj demon answered: "O holy, well-formed Sraosha! This is the thing that undoes it, namely, when a man unasked, kindly and piously, gives to one of the faithful something, be it ever so little, of the riches he has treasured up.

38. "He does thereby as thoroughly destroy the fruit of my womb as a four-footed wolf does, who tears the child out of a mother's womb."

39. The holy Sraosha, letting down his club upon her, asked the Druj: "O thou wretched, worthless Druj! Who is the second of those males of thine?"

40. The Druj demon answered: "O holy, well-formed Sraosha! He is the second of my males who, making water, lets it fall along the upper forepart of his foot.

41. "That man makes me conceive progeny as other males make their females conceive by their seed."

42. The holy Sraosha, letting his club down upon her, asked the Druj: "O thou wretched, worthless Druj! What is the thing that can undo that?"

43. The Druj demon answered: "O holy, well-formed Sraosha! This is the thing that undoes it, namely, when the man rising up and stepping three steps farther off, shall say three *Ahuna-Vairya,* two *humatanam,* three *hukhshathro-temam,* and then chant the *Ahuna-Vairya* and offer up one *Yenhe hatam.*

44. "He does thereby as thoroughly destroy the fruit of my womb as a four-footed wolf does, who tears the child out of a mother's womb."

45. The holy Sraosha, letting his club down upon her, asked the Druj: "O thou wretched, worthless Druj! Who is the third of those males of thine?"

46. The Druj demon answered: "O holy, well-formed Sraosha! He is the third of my males who during his sleep emits seed.

47. "That man makes me conceive progeny in the same manner as other males make their females conceive progeny by their seed."

48. The holy Sraosha, letting his club down upon her,

asked the Druj: "O thou wretched, worthless Druj! What is the thing that can undo that?"

49. The Druj demon answered: "O holy, well-formed Sraosha! this is the thing that undoes it, namely, if the man, when he has risen from sleep, shall say three *Ahuna-Vairya,* two *humatanam,* three *hukhshathrotemam,* and then chant the *Ahuna-Vairya,* and offer up one *Yenhe hatam.*

50. "He does thereby as thoroughly destroy the fruit of my womb as a four-footed wolf does who tears the child out of a mother's womb."

51. Then he shall speak unto Spenta Armaiti,[23] saying: "O Spenta Armaiti, this man do I deliver unto thee; this man deliver thou back unto me, against the happy day of resurrection; deliver him back as one who knows the Gathas, who knows the Yasna, and the revealed Law, a wise and clever man, who is Obedience incarnate.

52. "Then thou shalt call his name 'Fire-creature, Fire-seed, Fire-offspring, Fire-land,' or any name wherein is the word Fire." [24]

53. The holy Sraosha, letting his club down upon her, asked the Druj: "O thou wretched, worthless Druj! Who is the fourth of those males of thine?"

54. The Druj demon answered: "O holy, well-formed Sraosha! This one is my fourth male who, either man or woman, being more than fifteen years of age, walks without wearing the sacred girdle and the sacred shirt.

55. "At the fourth step we Daevas, at once, wither him even to the tongue and the marrow, and he goes thenceforth with power to destroy the world of Righteousness, and he destroys it like the *Yatus* and the *Zandas.*" [25]

56. The holy Sraosha, letting his club down upon her, asked the Druj: "O thou wretched, worthless Druj, what is the thing that can undo that?"

57. The Druj demon answered: "O holy, well-formed Sraosha! There is no means of undoing it;

[23] The Genius of the Earth.

[24] Atar, the Fire, is the ideal father of the son to be born, as Spenta Armaiti, the Earth, is his ideal mother.

[25] The *Yatu* is a sorcerer; the *Zanda* is an apostle of Ahriman.

58. " When a man or a woman, being more than fifteen years of age, walks without wearing the sacred girdle or the sacred shirt.

59. " At the fourth step we Daevas, at once, wither him even to the tongue and the marrow, and he goes thenceforth with power to destroy the world of Righteousness, and he destroys it like the *Yatus* and the *Zandas*."

## IV

60. Demand of me, thou upright one! of me who am the Maker, the most beneficent of all beings, the best knowing, the most pleased in answering what is asked of me; demand of me that thou mayst be the better, that thou mayst be the happier.

61. Zarathushtra asked Ahura Mazda: " Who grieves thee with the sorest grief? Who pains thee with the sorest pain? "

62. Ahura Mazda answered: " It is the Gahi,[26] O Spitama Zarathushtra! who mixes in her the seed of the faithful and the unfaithful, of the worshipers of Mazda and the worshipers of the Daevas, of the wicked and the righteous.

63. " Her looks dries up one-third of the mighty floods that run from the mountains, O Zarathushtra; her look withers one-third of the beautiful, golden-hued, growing plants, O Zarathushtra;

64. " Her look withers one-third of the strength of Spenta Armaiti;[27] and her touch withers in the faithful one-third of his good thoughts, of his good words, of his good deeds, one-third of his strength, of his victorious power, and of his holiness.

65. " Verily I say unto thee, O Spitama Zarathushtra! such creatures ought to be killed even more than gliding snakes, than howling wolves, than the wild she-wolf that falls upon the fold, or than the she-frog that falls upon the waters with her thousandfold brood."

[26] The courtezan, as an incarnation of the female demon Gahi.
[27] The earth.

## V

66. Demand of me, thou upright one! of me who am the Maker, the most beneficent of all beings, the best knowing, the most pleased in answering what is asked of me; demand of me that thou mayst be the better, that thou mayst be the happier.

67–68. Zarathushtra asked Ahura Mazda: "If a man shall come unto a woman who has the whites or sees blood, and he does so wittingly and knowingly, and she allows it wilfully, wittingly, and knowingly, what is the atonement for it, what is the penalty that he shall pay to atone for the deed they have done?"

69. Ahura Mazda answered: "If a man shall come unto a woman who has the whites or sees blood, and he does so wittingly and knowingly, and she allows it wilfully, wittingly, and knowingly;

70. "He shall slay a thousand head of small cattle; he shall godly and piously offer up to the fire the entrails thereof together with *Zaothra*-libations; he shall bring the shoulder-bones to the Good Waters.

71. "He shall godly and piously bring unto the fire a thousand loads of soft wood, of *Urvasna, Vohu-gaona, Vohu-kereti, Hadha-naepata,* or of any sweet-scented plant.

72. "He shall tie and consecrate a thousand bundles of *Baresma;* he shall godly and piously offer up to the Good Waters a thousand *Zaothra*-libations, together with the *Haoma* and the milk, cleanly prepared and well strained — cleanly prepared and well strained by a pious man, and mixed with the roots of the tree known as *Hadha-naepata.*

73. "He shall kill a thousand snakes of those that go upon the belly, two thousand of the other kind; he shall kill a thousand land-frogs and two thousand water-frogs; he shall kill a thousand corn-carrying ants and two thousand of the other kind.

74. "He shall throw thirty bridges over canals; he shall undergo a thousand stripes with the *Aspahe-astra,* a thousand stripes with the *Sraosho-karana.*[28]

[28] Five *tanafuhrs,* that is six thousand *dirhems.*

75. " This is the atonement, this is the penalty that he shall pay to atone for the deed that he has done.

76. " If he shall pay it, he makes himself a viaticum into the world of the holy ones; if he shall not pay it, he makes himself a viaticum into the world of the wicked, into that world, made of darkness, the offspring of darkness, which is Darkness' self." [29]

FARGARD XIX.[1]— (THE TEMPTING OF ZARATHUSHTRA)

[29] Compare Fargard v, 62.

[1] I. Angra Mainyu sends the demon Buiti to kill Zarathushtra: Zarathushtra sings aloud the Ahuna-Vairya, and the demon flies away, confounded by the sacred words and by the Glory of Zarathushtra (sections 1–3).

I a. Angra Mainyu himself attacks him and propounds riddles to be solved under pain of death. The Prophet rejects him with heavenly stones, given by Ahura, and announces to him that he will destroy his creation. The demon promises him the empire of the world if he adores him, as his ancestors have done, and abjures the religion of Mazda. Zarathushtra rejects his offers scornfully. He announces he will destroy him with the arms given by Ahura, namely, the sacrificial implements and the sacred words. Then he recites the *Tad thwa peresa*, that is to say the Gatha in which he asks Ahura for instruction on all the mysteries of the material and spiritual world (sections 4–10).

The rest of the Fargard contains specimens of the several questions asked by Zarathushtra and the answers given by Ahura. It is an abridgement of the Revelation (compare Yt. XXIV).

II (11–17). How to destroy the uncleanness born from a contact with the dead? — By invoking the Mazdean Religion. A series of invocations taught by Ahura and developed by Zarathushtra (15–16).

III (18–19). How to promote the prosperity of the creation? — By the rites of the Baresman.

IV (20–25). How to purify man and clothes defiled by the dead? — With *gomez*, water, and perfume.

V (26–34). On the remuneration of deeds after death; on the fate of the wicked and the righteous; the Kinvad bridge.

II a (34–42). Another series of invocations.

VI (43–47). The demons, dismayed by the birth of the Prophet, rush back into hell.

As may be seen from the preceding analysis, the essential parts of this Fargard are sections I and VI, the rest being an indefinite development. It appears also from section VI, that the attacks of Buiti and Angra Mainyu against Zarathushtra and the attempt to seduce him are supposed to take place at the moment when he was born, which is confirmed by the testimony of the Nask Varshtmansar.— West, " Pahlavi Texts," IV, 226 *seq.*

I

1. From the region of the north, from the regions of the north,[2] forth rushed Angra Mainyu, the deadly, the Daeva of the Daevas.[3] And thus spake the evil-doer Angra Mainyu, the deadly: "Druj, rush down and kill him," O holy Zarathushtra! The Druj came rushing along, the demon Buiti,[4] who is deceiving, unseen death.[5]

2. Zarathushtra chanted aloud the Ahuna-Vairya: "The will of the Lord is the law of righteousness. The gifts of Vohu-mano to the deeds done in this world for Mazda. He who relieves the poor makes Ahura king."

He offered the sacrifice to the good waters of the good Daitya! He recited the profession of the worshipers of Mazda!

The Druj dismayed, rushed away, the demon Buiti, who is deceiving, unseen death.

3. And the Druj said unto Angra Mainyu: "Thou tormenter, Angra Mainyu! I see no way to kill Spitama Zarathushtra, so great is the glory of the holy Zarathushtra."

Zarathushtra saw all this within his soul: "The wicked, the evil-doing Daevas (thought he) take counsel together for my death."

I a

4. Up started Zarathushtra, forward went Zarathushtra, unabated by Akem-mano, by the hardness of his malignant riddles;[6] he went swinging stones in his hand, stones as big as a house,[7] which he obtained from the Maker, Ahura Mazda, he the holy Zarathushtra.

[2] From hell.

[3] "The fiend of fiends," the arch-fiend.

[4] Buiti is identified by the Greater Bundahish with the *But*, the idol, worshiped by Budasp (a corruption of Bodhisattva). Buiti would be therefore a personification of Buddhism, which was flourishing in Eastern Iran in the two centuries before and after Christ.

[5] Idolatry being the death of the soul.

[6] This is a fragment of an old legend in which Zarathushtra and Angra Mainyu played respectively the parts of Œdipus and the Sphinx.

[7] The Commentary has, "Some say, those stones are the Ahuna-Vairya." If one keeps in mind how much the Mussulman legend of Ibrahim owes to the legend of Zoroaster, one may easily admit that this

" Whereat on this wide, round earth, whose ends lie afar, whereat dost thou swing those stones, thou who standest by the upper bank of the river Darega,[8] in the mansion of Pourusaspa?"[9]

5. Thus Zarathushtra answered Angra Mainyu: "O evil-doer, Angra Mainyu! I will smite the creation of the Daeva; I will smite the Nasu, a creature of the Daeva; I will smite the Pairika Knathaiti,[10] till the victorious Saoshyant come up to life[11] out of the lake Kasava,[12] from the region of the dawn, from the regions of the dawn."

6. Again to him said the Maker of the evil world, Angra Mainyu: "Do not destroy my creatures, O holy Zara-thushtra! Thou art the son of Pourusaspa;[13] by thy mother I was invoked.[14] Renounce the good Religion of the worshipers of Mazda, and thou shalt gain such a boon as Vadhaghna[15] gained, the ruler of the nations."

7. Spitama Zarathushtra said in answer: "No! never will I renounce the good Religion of the worshipers of Mazda, either for body or life, though they should tear away the breath!"

8. Again to him said the Maker of the evil world, Angra Mainyu: "By whose Word wilt thou strike, by whose Word wilt thou repel, by whose weapon will the good creatures strike and repel my creation, who am Angra Mainyu?"

9. Spitama Zarathushtra said in answer: "The sacred

passage in our text is the origin of the story of how Iblis tempted Ibrahim, and was pelted away, whence he was named "the stoned One."

[8] "The Daraga is the chief of the rivers, because the house of Zartusht's father stood on its bank and Zartusht was born there."— Bund. XXIV, 15.

[9] The father of Zarathushtra.

[10] The incarnation of idolatry.

[11] The unborn son of Zoroaster, who, at the end of time, will destroy Ahriman and bring about the resurrection of the dead.

[12] The Zarah sea in Saistan.

[13] "I know thee."— Commentary.

[14] The Commentary has, "Some explain thus: Thy forefathers wor-shiped me: worship me also." Zoroaster's forefathers must naturally have followed a false religion, since he announces the true one.

[15] Azi Dahaka or Zohak, who, as a legendary king, is said to have ruled the world for a thousand years.

mortar, the sacred cups, the *Haoma,* the Word taught by
Mazda — these are my weapons, my best weapons! By this
Word will I strike, by this Word will I repel, by this weapon
will the good creatures strike and repel thee, O evil-doer,
Angra Mainyu! The Good Spirit made the creation; [16] he
made it in the boundless Time. The Amesha-Spentas made
the creation, the good, the wise Sovereigns."

10. Zarathushtra chanted aloud the Ahuna-Vairya.

The holy Zarathushtra said aloud: "This I ask thee:
teach me the truth, O Lord! . . ."

## II

11. Zarathushtra asked Ahura Mazda: "O Ahura Mazda,
most beneficent spirit, Maker of the material world, thou
Holy One! [he was sitting by the upper bank of the Darega,
before Ahura Mazda, before the good Vohu-mano, before
Asha Vahista, Khshathra Vairya, and Spenta Armaiti;]

12. "How shall I free the world from that Druj, from
that evil-doer, Angra Mainyu? How shall I drive away
direct defilement? How indirect defilement? How shall
I drive the Nasu from the house of the worshipers of Mazda?
How shall I cleanse the faithful man? How shall I cleanse
the faithful woman?"

13. Ahura Mazda answered: "Invoke, O Zarathushtra!
the good Religion of Mazda.

"Invoke, O Zarathushtra! though thou see them not, the
Amesha-Spentas who rule over the seven *Karshvares* of the
earth.

"Invoke, O Zarathushtra! the sovereign Heaven, the
boundless Time,[17] and Vayu,[18] whose action is most high.

"Invoke, O Zarathushtra! the powerful Wind, made by
Mazda; and Spenta (Armaiti),[19] the fair daughter of Ahura
Mazda.

16 The first duty of every good Mazda-worshiper is to think of Ormazd
as the creator, and of Ahriman as the destroyer.— Minokhard II, 9.

17 By contradistinction to the duration of the world, which is limited
to 12,000 years.— Bund. xxxiv, 1.

18 The Genius of Destiny.

19 The fourth Amesha-Spenta, who in her spiritual character is an in-

14. "Invoke, O Zarathushtra! my Fravashi, who am Ahura Mazda, the greatest, the best, the fairest of all beings, the most solid, the most intelligent, the best shapen, the highest in holiness, and whose soul is the holy Word!

"Invoke, O Zarathushtra! this creation of mine, who am Ahura Mazda."

15. Zarathushtra imitated my words from me, and said: "I invoke the holy creation of Ahura Mazda.

"I invoke Mithra, the lord of the rolling country-side, a god armed with beautiful weapons, with the most glorious of all weapons, with the most victorious of all weapons.

"I invoke the holy, well-formed Sraosha, who wields a club in his hand, to bear upon the heads of the fiends.

16. "I invoke the most glorious Holy Word.

"I invoke the sovereign Heaven, the boundless Time, and Vayu, whose action is most high.

"I invoke the mighty Wind, made by Mazda, and Spenta (Armaiti), the fair daughter of Ahura Mazda.

"I invoke the good Religion of Mazda, the fiend-destroying Law of Zarathushtra."

## III

17. Zarathushtra asked Ahura Mazda: "O Maker of the good world, Ahura Mazda! With what manner of sacrifice shall I worship, with what manner of sacrifice shall I make people worship this creation of Ahura Mazda?"

18. Ahura Mazda answered: "Go, O Spitama Zarathushtra! toward the high-growing trees, and before one of them that is beautiful, high-growing, and mighty, say thou these words: 'Hail to thee! O good, holy tree, made by Mazda! *Ashem vohu!*'"

19. "The priest shall cut off a twig of *Baresma*, long as an *aesha*, thick as a *yava*. The faithful one, holding it in his left hand, shall keep his eyes upon it without ceasing, whilst he is offering up to Ahura Mazda and to the Amesha-Spentas, the high and beautiful golden *Haomas*, and Good

carnation of pious humility and in her material character the Genius of the Earth.

Thought and the good Rata,[20] made by Mazda, holy and excellent."

## IV

20. Zarathushtra asked Ahura Mazda: "O thou, all-knowing Ahura Mazda! thou art never asleep, never intoxicated, thou Ahura Mazda! Vohu-mano [21] gets directly defiled: Vohu-mano gets indirectly defiled; the Daevas defile him from the bodies smitten by the Daevas: let Vohu-mano be made clean."

21. Ahura Mazda answered: "Thou shalt take some *gomez* from a bull ungelded and such as the law requires it. Thou shalt take the man who is to be cleansed to the field made by Ahura, and the man that is to cleanse him shall draw the furrows.

22. "He shall recite a hundred *Ashem vohu:* 'Holiness is the best of all good: it is also happiness. Happy the man who is holy with perfect holiness!'"

"He shall chant two hundred Ahuna-Vairya: 'The will of the Lord is the law of righteousness. The gifts of Vohu-mano to the deeds done in this world for Mazda! He who relieves the poor makes Ahura king.'

"He shall wash himself four times with the *gomez* from the ox, and twice with the water made by Mazda.

23. "Thus Vohu-mano shall be made clean, and clean shall be the man. The man shall take up Vohu-mano with the left arm and the right, with the right arm and the left: and thou shalt lay down Vohu-mano under the mighty light of the heavens, by the light of the stars made by the gods, until nine nights have passed away.

[20] Rata impersonates the liberalities done by men to God (as offerings) and by God to men (as riches, etc.).

[21] Vohu-mano is often used as a designation of the faithful one, literally, "the good-minded"; this is the meaning which is given to it in this passage by the Commentary, and it certainly belongs to it in the second part of section 25; but in the first part of the same clause it is translated "clothes," a meaning which is not unlikely in itself, as Vohu-mano, being the Amshaspand of cattle, may designate, and in fact did designate, the skins of cattle and leather.— Commentary ad Fargard XVIII, 2. On the whole the description in the text applies to the cleans-

24. "When nine nights have passed away, thou shalt bring libations unto the fire, thou shalt bring hard wood unto the fire, thou shalt bring incense of Vohu-gaona unto the fire, and thou shalt perfume Vohu-mano therewith.

25. "Thus shall Vohu-mano be made clean, and clean shall be the man. He shall take up Vohu-mano with the right arm and the left, with the left arm and the right, and Vohu-mano shall say aloud: 'Glory be to Ahura Mazda! Glory be to the Amesha-Spentas! Glory be to all the other holy beings.'"

### V.

26. Zarathushtra asked Ahura Mazda: "O thou all-knowing Ahura Mazda: Should I urge upon the godly man, should I urge upon the godly woman, should I urge upon the wicked Daeva-worshiper who lives in sin, to give the earth made by Ahura, the water that runs, the corn that grows, and all the rest of their wealth?"

Ahura Mazda answered: "Thou shouldst, O holy Zarathushtra."

27. O Maker of the material world, thou Holy One! Where are the rewards given? Where does the rewarding take place? Where is the rewarding fulfilled? Whereto do men come to take the reward that, during their life in the material world, they have won for their souls?

28. Ahura Mazda answered: "When the man is dead, when his time is over, then the wicked, evil-doing Daevas cut off his eyesight. On the third night, when the dawn appears and brightens up, when Mithra, the god with beautiful weapons, reaches the all-happy mountains, and the sun is rising:

29. "Then the fiend, named Vizaresha,[22] O Spitama Zarathushtra, carries off in bonds [23] the souls of the wicked

ing both of the man and of the clothes, and Vohu-mano sometimes means the one, and sometimes the other.

[22] The demon Vizaresh is he who, during that struggle of three days and three nights with the souls of the departed, carries terror on them and beats them: he sits at the gate of hell.— Bund. xxviii, 18.

[23] "Every one has a noose cast around his neck: when a man dies, if he has been a righteous man, the noose falls from his neck; if a wicked,

Daeva-worshipers who live in sin. The soul enters the way made by Time, and open both to the wicked and to the righteous. At the head of the Kinvad bridge, the holy bridge made by Mazda, they ask for their spirits and souls the reward for the worldly goods which they gave away here below.

30. "Then comes the beautiful, well-shapen, strong and well-formed maid, with the dogs at her sides, one who can distinguish, who has many children, happy, and of high understanding.

"She makes the soul of the righteous one go up above the Hara-berezaiti; above the Kinvad bridge she places it in the presence of the heavenly gods themselves.

31. "Up rises Vohu-mano [24] from his golden seat; Vohu-mano exclaims: 'How hast thou come to us, thou Holy One, from that decaying world into this undecaying one?'

32. "Gladly pass the souls of the righteous to the golden seat of Ahura Mazda, to the golden seat of the Amesha-Spentas, to the Garo-nmanem,[25] the abode of Ahura Mazda, the abode of the Amesha-Spentas, the abode of all the other holy beings.

33. "As to the godly man that has been cleansed, the wicked, evil-doing Daevas tremble at the perfume of his soul after death, as doth a sheep on which a wolf is pouncing.[26]

34. "The souls of the righteous are gathered together there: Nairyo-sangha is with them; a messenger of Ahura Mazda is Nairyo-sangha.

## II a

"Invoke, O Zarathushtra! this very creation of Ahura Mazda."

they drag him with that noose down into hell."— Commentary; compare Fargard v, 8.

[24] The doorkeeper of Paradise.

[25] The *Garothman* of the Parsis; literally, "the house of songs"; it is the highest Paradise.

[26] Ormazd is all perfume, Ahriman is infection and stench (Bundahis I; Eznig, Refutatio Haeresiarum II); the souls of their followers partake of the same qualities, and by the performance of the Barashnum both the body and the soul are perfumed and sweetened.

35. Zarathushtra imitated those words of mine: " I invoke the holy world, made by Ahura Mazda.

" I invoke the earth made by Ahura, the water made by Mazda, the holy trees.

" I invoke the sea Vouru-kasha.

" I invoke the beautiful Heaven.[27]

" I invoke the endless and sovereign Light.[28]

36. " I invoke the bright, blissful Paradise of the Holy Ones.

" I invoke the Garo-nmanem, the abode of Ahura Mazda, the abode of the Amesha-Spentas, the abode of all the other holy beings.

" I invoke the sovereign Place of Eternal Weal,[29] and the Kinvad bridge made by Mazda.

37. " I invoke the good Saoka,[30] who has the good eye.

" I invoke the whole creation of weal.

" I invoke the mighty Fravashis of the righteous.

" I invoke Verethraghna,[31] made by Ahura, who wears the Glory made by Mazda.

" I invoke Tistrya,[32] the bright and glorious star, in the shape of a golden-horned bull.[33]

38. " I invoke the holy, beneficent Gathas, who rule over the *Ratus:*[34]

[27] Asman, the highest heaven, as distinguished from the firmament (*thwasha*) that lies nearer the earth.

[28] The endless Light is " the place of Ormazd " (Bund. I); it is Infinite Space conceived as luminous.

[29] *Misvana gatva*, another name of the heavenly spaces; it designates heaven as the abode and source of all blessings, of all *savah*, or *saoka*.

[30] A Genius defined, " Genius of the good eye," by opposition to " the bad eye." Saoka (*Sok*) is an auxiliary to Mithra (*Mihr*); she receives first, from above, all the good destined to man, and transmits it to the lower sky or firmament (which is the seat of Destiny) through the moon and Ardvisur.— Gr. Bund.

[31] The Genius of Victory (Bahram).

[32] Tistrya (*Tir*), the star of rain.

[33] Tistrya appears successively under three forms, during the month named from him (the first month of summer, June 21–July 21): ten days as a man, ten days as a bull, ten days as a horse. " As a bull he is most to be invoked " (Commentary), to prepare has final victory over the demon of Drought, Apaosha.

[34] The chiefs of creation; " they rule over the *Ratus* inasmuch as it is by their means that these other *Ratus* are invoked."— Commentary.

"I invoke the Ahunavaiti Gatha;

"I invoke the Ustavaiti Gatha;

"I invoke the Spenta-mainyu Gatha;

"I invoke the Vohu-khshathra Gatha;

"I invoke the Vahistoisti Gatha.

39. "I invoke the Karshvares of Arzahe and Savahe;

"I invoke the Karshvares of Fradadhafshu and Vida-dhafshu;

"I invoke the Karshvares of Vourubaresti and Vouru-zaresti;

"I invoke the bright Hvaniratha; [35]

"I invoke the bright, glorious Haetumant;

"I invoke the good Ashi; [36]

"I invoke the good Kisti; [37]

"I invoke the most pure Kista; [38]

"I invoke the Glory of the Aryan regions; [39]

"I invoke the Glory of the bright Yima, the good shepherd.

40. "Let him be worshiped with sacrifice, let him be gladdened, gratified, and satisfied, the holy Sraosha, the well-formed, victorious, holy Sraosha.[40]

"Bring libations unto the Fire, bring hard wood unto the Fire, bring incense of Vohu-gaona unto the Fire.

"Offer up the sacrifice to the Vazista fire,[41] which smites the fiend Spengaghra: [42] bring unto it the cooked meat and full overflowing libations.

41. "Offer up the sacrifice to the holy Sraosha, that the holy Sraosha may smite down the fiend Kunda, who is

[35] The earth is divided into seven Karshvares, of which the central one, Hvaniratha, is the finest and contains Iran.

[36] Ashi (Ashishvang), the Genius that imparts riches to the righteous.

[37] An angel of religious knowledge.

[38] Religious knowledge: invoked with Daena.— Religion; Siroza, 24.

[39] The light of sovereignty, *hvareno*, which if secured by the Aryans makes them rule over their enemies.

[40] That he may smite Aeshma and the other fiends.

[41] The fire of lightning.

[42] The demon that prevents the fall of rain; a companion in arms of Apaosha.

drunken without drinking,[43] and throws down into the Hell of the Druj the wicked Daeva-worshipers, who live in sin.

42. " I invoke the Kara fish, who lives beneath waters in the bottom of the deep lakes.

" I invoke the ancient and sovereign Merezu,[44] the most warlike of the creatures of the two Spirits.

" I invoke the seven bright Sru . . ."

## VI

43. " They cried about, their minds wavered to and fro,[45] Angra Mainyu the deadly, the Daeva of the Daevas; Indra the Daeva, Sauru the Daeva, Naunghaithya the Daeva, Taurvi and Zairi; Aeshma of the murderous spear; Akatasha the Daeva; Winter, made by the Daevas; the deceiving, unseen Death; Zaurva,[46] baneful to the fathers; Buiti the Daeva; Driwi [47] the Daeva; Daiwi [48] the Daeva; Kasvi [49] the Daeva; Paitisha [50] the most Daeva-like amongst the Daevas.

44. " And the evil-doing Daeva, Angra Mainyu, the deadly, said: ' What! let the wicked, evil-doing Daevas gather together at the head of Arezura! ' [51]

45. " They rush away shouting, the wicked, evil-doing Daevas; they run away shouting, the wicked, evil-doing Daevas; they run away casting the Evil Eye, the wicked, evil-doing Daevas: ' Let us gather together at the head of Arezura!

46. " ' For he is just born the holy Zarathushtra, in the house of Pourusaspa.  How can we procure his death?  He

[43] Whereas Aeshma, the other arch-enemy of Sraosha, borrows part of his strength from drunkenness.

[44] From its two epithets, " ancient" and " sovereign," it appears that it must designate one of the first principles, that is to say, some form of Heaven, Light, Space, or Time.

[45] Up and down, in hope and despair.

[46] Old age.

[47] Malice; see Fargard II.

[48] Lying.

[49] Spite.

[50] Opposition, or counter-action, the same as Paityara; a personification of the doings of Ahriman and of his marring power.

[51] At the gate of hell.

is the weapon that fells the fiends: he is a counter-fiend to
the fiends; he is a Druj to the Druj. Vanished are the
Daeva-worshipers, the Nasu made by the Daeva, the false-
speaking Lie! '

47. "They rush away shouting, the wicked, evil-doing
Daevas, into the depths of the dark, raging world of hell.

"*Ashem vohu:* Holiness is the best of all good."

## FARGARD XX.— (ON MEDICINE)

### THRITA, THE FIRST HEALER [1]

1. Zarathushtra asked Ahura Mazda: "Ahura Mazda,
most beneficent Spirit, Maker of the material world, thou
Holy one! Who was he who first of the healers,[2] of the
wise, the happy, the wealthy, the glorious, the strong, the
Paradhatas,[3] drove back sickness to sickness, drove back
death to death; [4] and first turned away the point of the
sword and the fire of fever from the bodies of mortals? "

2. Ahura Mazda answered: "Thrita it was who first of
the healers, of the wise, the happy, the wealthy, the glorious,
the strong, the Paradhatas, drove back sickness to sickness,
drove back death to death, and first turned away the point
of the sword and the fire of fever from the bodies of mortals.

3. "He asked for a source of remedies; he obtained it

[1] The Parsis say there are three kinds of medicine: one that heals
with the knife, one that heals with herbs, and one that heals with sacred
spells. The present Fargard deals with the origin of medicine, particu-
larly the herbs-medicine. Its inventor was Thrita, of the Sama family,
to whom Ahura Mazda brought down from heaven ten thousand healing
plants that had been growing up around the tree of eternal life, the
white *Hom* or *Gaokerena* (section 4). This Thrita is mentioned only
once again in the Avesta, in Yasna IX, where he appears to have been
one of the first priests of *Haoma.* This accounts for his medical skill;
as *Haoma* is the plant of eternal life, it is but natural that one of his
first priests should have been the first healer.

This Fargard has only an allusion to the origin of the knife-medicine,
which was, as it seems, revealed by Khshathra Vairya (section 3). The
last paragraphs (sections 5–12) deal with the spell-medicine.

[2] "Those who knew how to take care of their own bodies, like
Isfandyar: some say that no sword could wound him."— Commentary.

[3] The Paradhata or *Peshdad*, the kings of the first Iranian dynasty.

[4] "That is to say, who kept sickness in bonds, who kept death in
bonds."— Commentary.

from Khshathra-Vairya,[5] to withstand sickness and to withstand death; to withstand pain and to withstand fever; to
withstand *Sarana* and to withstand *Sarastya;*[6] to withstand
*Azana* and to withstand *Azahva;* to withstand *Kurugha* and
to withstand *Azivaka;* to withstand *Duruka* and to withstand
*Astairya;* to withstand the evil eye, rottenness, and infection
which Angra Mainyu had created against the bodies of
mortals.

4. "And I, Ahura Mazda, brought down the healing
plants that, by many hundreds, by many thousands, by many
myriads, grow up all around the one *Gaokerena.*[7]

5. "All this do we achieve; all this do we order; all these
prayers do we utter, for the benefit of the bodies of mortals;[8]

6. "To withstand sickness and to withstand death; to
withstand pain and to withstand fever; to withstand *Sarana*
and to withstand *Sarastya;* to withstand *Azana* and to with-
stand *Azahva;* to withstand *Kurugha* and to withstand *Azivaka;* to withstand *Duruka* and to withstand *Astairya;* to
withstand the evil eye, rottenness, and infection which Angra
Mainyu has created against the bodies of mortals.

7. "To thee, O Sickness, I say avaunt! to thee, O Death,
I say avaunt! to thee, O Pain, I say avaunt! to thee, O
Fever, I say avaunt! to thee, O Evil Eye, I say avaunt! to

5 As Khshathra-Vairya presides over metals, it was a knife he
received, " of which the point and the base were set in gold." He
was therefore the first who healed with the knife, as well as the first who
healed with herbs. As for the healing with the holy word, see sections
5 and *seq.*

6 Headache and cold fever.

7 There are two *Haomas:* one is the yellow or golden *Haoma,* which
is the earthly *Haoma,* and which, when prepared for the sacrifice, is the
king of healing plants; the other is the white *Haoma* or *Gaokerena,* which
grows up in the middle of the sea Vouru-Kasha, where it is surrounded
by the ten thousand healing plants created by Ormazd in order to oppose
so many diseases that had been created by Ahriman. A frog goes
swimming around the *Gaokerena* to gnaw it down: but two Kar Mahi
(Fargard XIX, 42) keep watch and circle around the tree, so that the
head of one of them is continually toward the frog.— Bund. XVIII.

8 " We do all that is necessary for healing; we give, as Dastobar (Das-
tur), the necessary prescriptions; we recite the needed prayers."— This
section is a transition to the spell-medicine.

thee, O *Sarana*, I say avaunt! and to thee, O *Sarastya*, I say
avaunt! to thee, O *Azana*, I say avaunt! and to thee, O
*Azahva*, I say avaunt! to thee, O *Kurugha*, I say avaunt!
and to thee, O *Azivaka*, I say avaunt! to thee, O *Duruka*,
I say avaunt! and to thee, O *Astairya*, I say avaunt!

8. "Give us, O Ahura, that powerful sovereignty, by the
strength of which we may smite down the Druj! By its
might may we smite the Druj!

9. "I drive away *Ishire* and I drive away *Aghuire;* I
drive away *Aghra* and I drive away *Ughra;* I drive away
sickness and I drive away death; I drive away pain and I
drive away fever; I drive away *Sarana* and I drive away
*Sarastya;* I drive away *Azana* and I drive away *Azahva;*
I drive away *Kurugha* and I drive away *Azivaka;* I drive
away *Duruka* and I drive away *Astairya;* I drive away the
evil eye, rottenness, and infection which Angra Mainyu has
created against the bodies of mortals.

10. "I drive away all manner of sickness and death, all
the Yatus and Pairikas, and all the wicked Gainis.

11. "*A Airyama ishyo.* May the vow-fulfilling Airyaman come here, for the men and women of Zarathushtra to
rejoice, for Vohu-mano to rejoice; with the desirable reward
that Religion deserves. I solicit for holiness that boon that
is vouchsafed by Ahura!

12. "May the vow-fulfilling Airyaman smite all manner
of sickness and death, all the Yatus and Pairikas, and all
the wicked Gainis."

13. *Yatha ahu vairyo:* The will of the Lord is the law of
righteousness.

The gifts of Vohu-mano to the deeds done in this world
for Mazda. He who relieves the poor makes Ahura king.

*Kem-na mazda:* What protector hast thou given unto me,
O Mazda! while the hate of the wicked encompasses me?
Whom but thy Atar and Vohu-mano, through whose work
I keep on the world of Righteousness? Reveal therefore to
me thy Religion as thy rule!

*Ke verethrem-ga:* Who is the victorious who will protect

thy teaching? Make it clear that I am the guide for both worlds. May Sraosha come with Vohu-mano and help whomsoever thou pleasest, O Mazda!

Keep us from our hater, O Mazda and Armaiti Spenta; Perish, O fiendish Druj! Perish, O brood of the fiend! Perish, O world of the fiend! Perish away, O Druj! Perish away to the regions of the north, never more to give unto death the living world of Righteousness!

### FARGARD XXI.— (HYMNS AND CHARMS)
#### I

1. Hail, bounteous bull![1] Hail to thee, beneficent bull! Hail to thee, who makest increase! Hail to thee, who makest growth! Hail to thee, who dost bestow his part[2] upon the righteous faithful, and wilt bestow it on the faithful yet unborn! Hail to thee, whom the Gahi kills,[3] and the ungodly *Ashemaogha,* and the wicked tyrant.[4]

#### II

2. "Come, come on, O clouds, from up above, down on the earth, by thousands of drops, by myriads of drops": thus say, O holy Zarathushtra! "to destroy sickness, to destroy death, to destroy the sickness that kills, to destroy death that kills, to destroy Gadha and Apagadha.[5]

3. "If death come after noon, may healing come at eve!

"If death come at eve, may healing come at night!

"If death come at night, may healing come at dawn!

"And showers shower down new water, new earth, new plants, new healing powers, and new healing.

#### III a

4. "As the sea Vouru-kasha is the gathering-place of the

[1] The primeval bull who was created by Ormazd and killed by Ahriman with the help of the Gahi. Clause 1 is to be recited when one meets an ox or any kind of cattle.— Gr. Rav. 386.

[2] Possibly, "who dost kill the Gahi."

[3] His daily food.

[4] The wicked kills animals, out of mere cruelty, beyond his needs.

[5] Names of diseases.

waters,[6] rising up and going down, up the aerial way and down the earth, down the earth and up the aerial way: thus rise up and roll along! thou in whose rising and growing Ahura Mazda made the aerial way.

5. "Up! rise up and roll along! thou swift-horsed Sun, above Hara Berezaiti, and produce light for the world, and mayst thou, O man! rise up there, if thou art to abide in Garo-nmanem, along the path made by Mazda, along the way made by the gods, the watery way they opened.

6. "And the Holy Word shall keep away the evil: Of thee, O child! I will cleanse the birth and growth; of thee, O woman! I will make the body and the strength pure; I will make thee rich in children and rich in milk;

7. "Rich in seed, in milk,[7] in fat, in marrow, and in offspring. I shall bring to thee a thousand pure springs, running toward the pastures that give food to the child.

## III b

8. "As the sea Vouru-kasha is the gathering-place of the waters, rising up and going down, up the aerial way and down the earth, down the earth and up the aerial way:

"Thus rise up and roll along! thou in whose rising and growing Ahura Mazda made the earth.

9. "Up! rise up, thou Moon, that dost keep in thee the seed of the bull;[8]

[6] Waters and light are believed to flow from the same spring and in the same bed: "As the light comes in through Alborz (Hara Berezaiti) and goes out through Alborz, so water also comes out through Alborz and goes away through Alborz."— Bund. xx, 4. Every day the sun, moon, and stars rise up from Alborz, and every day all the waters on earth come back together to the sea Vouru-kasha, and there collected come down again to the earth from the peaks of Alborz.— Gr. Rav. 431. As light comes from three different sources (the sun, the moon, and the stars), the waters are invoked three times, first in company with the sun, then with the moon, lastly with the stars, as if there should be three different movements of the rain connected with the three movements of light.

[7] There are, in the text, two words for "milk," the one referring to the milk of women, the other to the milk of cows.

[8] When the primeval bull died, "what was bright and strong in his seed was brought to the sphere of the moon, and when it was cleansed

" Rise up above Hara Berezaiti, and produce light for the
world, and mayst thou, O man! rise up there, if thou art to
abide in Garo-nmanem, along the path made by Mazda, along
the way made by the gods, the watery way they opened.

10. " And the Holy Word shall keep away the evil: Of
thee, O child! I will cleanse the birth and growth; of thee,
O woman! I will make the body and the strength pure; I
make thee rich in children and rich in milk;

11. " Rich in seed, in milk, in fat, in marrow, and in offspring. I shall bring to thee a thousand pure springs, running toward the pastures that give food to the child.

## III c

12. " As the sea Vouru-kasha is the gathering-place of the
waters, rising up and going down, up the aerial way and
down the earth, down the earth and up the aerial way:

" Thus rise up and roll along; thou in whose rising and
growing Ahura Mazda made everything that grows.[9]

13. " Up! rise up, ye deep Stars, that have in you the
seed of waters;

" Rise up above Hara Berezaiti, and produce light for the
world, and mayst thou, O man! rise up there, if thou art to
abide in Garo-nmanem, along the path made by Mazda, along
the way made by the gods, the watery way they opened.

14. " And the Holy Word shall keep away the evil: Of
thee, O child! I will cleanse the birth and growth; of thee,
O woman! I will make the body and the strength pure; I
make thee rich in children and rich in milk;

15. " Rich in seed, in milk, in fat, in marrow, and in offspring. I shall bring to thee a thousand pure springs, running toward the pastures that will give food to the child.

16. " As the sea Vouru-kasha is the gathering-place of the
waters, rising up and going down, up the aerial way and
down the earth, down the earth and up the aerial way:

there in the light of the astre, two creatures were shaped with it, a male
and a female, from which came two hundred and seventy-two kinds of
animals."— Bund. IV, x.

⁹ The plants that grow under the action of " those stars that have in
them the seed of waters " (compare section 13).

" Thus rise up and roll along! ye in whose rising and growing Ahura Mazda made everything that rises.

17. " In your rising away will the Kahvuzi [10] fly and cry, away will the Ayehi [11] fly and cry, away will the Gahi, who follows the Yatu, fly and cry.

## IV

18. " I drive away Ishire and I drive away Aghuire; I drive away Aghra and I drive away Ughra; I drive away sickness and I drive away death; I drive away pain and I drive away fever; I drive away *Sarana* and I drive away *Sarastya*. I drive away *Azana* and I drive away *Azahva;* I drive away *Kurugha* and I drive away *Azivaka;* I drive away *Duruka* and I drive away *Astairya;* I drive away the evil eye, rottenness, and infection which Angra Mainyu has created against the bodies of mortals.

19. " I drive away all manner of sickness and death, all the Yatus and Pairikas, and all the wicked Gainis.

20. " *A Airyama ishyo:* May the vow-fulfilling Airyaman come here, for the men and women of Zarathushtra to rejoice, for Vohu-mano to rejoice; with the desirable reward that Religion deserves. I solicit for holiness that boon that is vouchsafed by Ahura!

21. " May the vow-fulfilling Airyaman smite all manner of sickness and death, all the Yatus and Pairikas, and all the wicked Gainis.

22. " *Yatha ahu vairyo:* The will of the Lord is the law of righteousness!

" *Kem-na mazda:* What protector hast thou given unto me . . . ?

" *Ke verethrem-ga:* Who is the victorious who will protect thy teaching . . . ?

23. " Keep us from our hater, O Mazda and Armaiti Spenta! Perish, O fiendish Druj! Perish, O brood of the fiend! Perish, O world of the fiend! Perish away, O Druj! Perish away to the regions of the north, never more to give unto death the living world of Righteousness! "

[10] " He who diminishes glory, Ahriman."— Commentary.
[11] " Sterility, Ahriman."— Commentary.

FARGARD XXII.[1]— (THE SPELL AGAINST SICKNESS)

## I

1. Ahura Mazda spake unto Spitama Zarathushtra, saying: "I, Ahura Mazda, the Maker of all good things, when I made this mansion,[2] the beautiful, the shining, seen afar (there may I go up, there may I arrive!).

2. "Then the ruffian looked at me;[3] the ruffian Angra Mainyu, the deadly, wrought against me nine diseases, and ninety, and nine hundred, and nine thousand, and nine times ten thousand diseases. So mayst thou heal me, thou most glorious Mathra Spenta!

3. "Unto thee will I give in return a thousand fleet, swift-running steeds; I offer thee up a sacrifice, O good Saoka,[4] made by Mazda and holy.

"Unto thee will I give in return a thousand fleet, high-humped camels; I offer thee up a sacrifice, O good Saoka, made by Mazda and holy.

4. "Unto thee will I give in return a thousand brown oxen that do not push; I offer thee up a sacrifice, O good Saoka, made by Mazda and holy.

"Unto thee will I give in return a thousand females big with young, of all species of small cattle; I offer thee up a sacrifice, O good Saoka, made by Mazda and holy.

[1] It has already been seen that, of all healers, the most powerful is the one who treats with the Holy Word (Mathra Spenta), that is with sacred spells. Of all sacred spells, the most efficacious is the *Airyama ishyo*. This is expressed under a mythological form in this Fargard.

Angra Mainyu having created 99,999 diseases, Ahura applies for remedy to the Holy Word (Mathra Spenta; sections 1-5).— How shall I manage? asks Mathra Spenta (section 16). Ahura sends his messenger to Airyaman with the same request. Airyaman comes at once to Ahura's call, and digs nine furrows. It is no doubt in order to perform the Barashnum, by the virtue of which the strength of the demon and of the demon's work will be broken. The Fargard ends therefore with spells against sickness and against death, added to the usual spells of the ordinary Barashnum.

[2] "The *Garotman*."— Commentary. Paradise.

[3] And cast on me the evil eye; "it was by casting the evil eye on the good creatures of Ormazd that Ahriman corrupted them." Compare Fargard xx, 3.

[4] The Genius of the good eye.

5. "And I will bless thee with the fair blessing-spell of the righteous, the friendly blessing-spell of the righteous, that makes the empty swell to fulness and the full to overflowing, that comes to help him who was sickening, and makes the sick man sound again.

6. "Mathra Spenta, the all-glorious, replied unto me: 'How shall I heal thee? How shall I drive away from thee those nine diseases, and those ninety, those nine hundred, those nine thousand, and those nine times ten thousand diseases?'"

## II

7. The Maker Ahura Mazda called for Nairyo-sangha:[5] Go thou, Nairyo-sangha, the herald, and drive toward the mansion of Airyaman, and speak thus unto him:

8. Thus speaks Ahura Mazda, the Holy One, unto thee: "I, Ahura Mazda, the Maker of all good things, when I made this mansion, the beautiful, the shining, seen afar (there may I ascend, there may I arrive!).

9. "Then the ruffian looked at me; the ruffian Angra Mainyu, the deadly, wrought against me nine diseases, and ninety, and nine hundred, and nine thousand, and nine times ten thousand diseases. So mayst thou heal me, O Airyaman, the vow-fulfiller!

10. "Unto thee will I give in return a thousand fleet, swift-running steeds; I offer thee up a sacrifice, O good Saoka, made by Mazda and holy.

"Unto thee will I give in return a thousand fleet, high-humped camels; I offer thee up a sacrifice, O good Saoka, made by Mazda and holy.

11. "Unto thee will I give in return a thousand brown oxen that do not push; I offer thee up a sacrifice, O good Saoka, made by Mazda and holy.

"Unto thee will I give in return a thousand females big with young, of all species of small cattle. I offer thee up a sacrifice, O good Saoka, made by Mazda and holy.

12. "And I will bless thee with the fair blessing-spell of

[5] The messenger of Ahura Mazda. He is a form of Atar, the Fire.

the righteous, the friendly blessing-spell of the righteous, that makes the empty swell to fulness and the full to overflowing, that comes to help him who was sickening, and makes the sick man sound again."

## III

13. In obedience to Ahura's words he went, Nairyo-sangha, the herald; he drove toward the mansion of Airyaman, he spake unto Airyaman, saying:

14. Thus speaks Ahura Mazda, the Holy One, unto thee: " I, Ahura Mazda, the Maker of all good things, when I made this mansion, the beautiful, the shining, seen afar (there may I go up, there may I arrive!).

15. " Then the ruffian looked at me; the ruffian Angra Mainyu, the deadly, wrought against me nine diseases, and ninety, and nine hundred, and nine thousand, and nine times ten thousand diseases. So mayest thou heal me, O Airyaman, the vow-fulfiller!

16. " Unto thee will I give in return a thousand fleet, swift-running steeds; I offer thee up a sacrifice, O good Saoka, made by Mazda and holy.

" Unto thee will I give in return a thousand fleet, high-humped camels; I offer thee up a sacrifice, O good Saoka, made by Mazda and holy.

17. " Unto thee will I give in return a thousand brown oxen that do not push; I offer thee up a sacrifice, O good Saoka, made by Mazda and holy.

" Unto thee will I give in return a thousand females, big with young, of all species of small cattle; I offer thee up a sacrifice, O good Saoka, made by Mazda and holy.

18. " And I will bless thee with the fair blessing-spell of the righteous, the friendly blessing-spell of the righteous, that makes the empty swell to fulness and the full to overflowing, that comes to help him who was sickening, and makes the sick man sound again."

## IV

19. Quickly was it done, nor was it long, eagerly set off

the vow-fulfilling Airyaman, toward the mountain of the holy Questions,[6] toward the forest of the holy Questions.

20. Nine kinds of stallions brought he with him, the vow-fulfilling Airyaman.[7]

Nine kinds of camels brought he with him, the vow-fulfilling Airyaman.

Nine kinds of bulls brought he with him, the vow-fulfilling Airyaman.

Nine kinds of small cattle brought he with him, the vow-fulfilling Airyaman.

He brought with him the nine twigs; he drew along nine furrows.

21. "I drive away Ishire and I drive away Aghuire; I drive away Aghra and I drive away Ughra; I drive away sickness and I drive away death; I drive away pain and I drive away fever; I drive away *Sarana* and I drive away *Sarastya;* I drive away *Azana,* and I drive away *Azahva;* I I drive away *Kurugha* and I drive away *Azivaka;* I drive away *Duruka* and I drive away *Astairya.* I drive away the evil eye, rottenness, and infection which Angra Mainyu has created against the bodies of mortals.

22. "I drive away all manner of sickness and death, all the Yatus and Pairikas, and all the wicked Gainis.

23. "May the vow-fulfilling Airyaman come here, for the men and women of Zarathushtra to rejoice, for Vohu-mano to rejoice; with the desirable reward that Religion deserves. I solicit for holiness that boon that is vouchsafed by Ahura.

24. "May the vow-fulfilling Airyaman smite all manner of sickness and death, all the Yatus and Pairikas, and all the wicked Gainis.

25. "*Yatha ahu vairyo:* The will of the Lord is the law of righteousness. The gifts of Vohu-mano to the deeds done in this world for Mazda. He who relieves the poor makes Ahura king.

[6] The mountain where "the holy conversations" between Ormazd and Zoroaster took place.

[7] According to Framji, "He brought with him the strength of nine stallions," to infuse it into the sick man.

"*Kem-na mazda:* What protector hast thou given unto me, O Mazda! while the hate of the wicked encompasses me? Whom but thy Atar and Vohu-mano, through whose work I keep on the world of righteousness? Reveal therefore to me thy Religion as thy rule!

"*Ke verethrem-ga:* Who is the victorious who will protect thy teaching? Make it clear that I am the guide for both worlds. May Sraosha come with Vohu-mano and help whomsoever thou pleasest, O Mazda!

"Keep us from our hater, O Mazda and Armaiti Spenta! Perish, O fiendish Druj! Perish, O brood of the fiend! Perish, O world of the fiend! Perish away, O Druj! Perish away to the regions of the north, never more to give unto death the living world of Righteousness!"

END OF THE VENDIDAD

www.ingramcontent.com/pod-product-compliance
Lightning Source LLC
Chambersburg PA
CBHW021109090426
42738CB00006B/573